RAILWAYS OF CORNWALL
A DECADE OF CHANGE

PART 1: The Cornish Main Line – Saltash to Penzance

KEITH BARROW

Front Cover: 43092 *Cromwell's Castle* leads 2C29, the 15.47 Plymouth–Penzance at Hallenbeagle level crossing, Scorrier, on 21 June 2023. **Keith Barrow**

Back cover: With DB Cargo-liveried 66009 dead-in-train, 66133 crosses St Pinnock Viaduct between Liskeard and Bodmin Parkway with the 6V99 Exeter Riverside–St Blazey empty china clay JIAs on 21 October 2021. **Keith Barrow**

Title page: 66015 crosses Largin Viaduct with 6C12, the Burngullow–Exeter Riverside sand train on 19 September 2019. **Nathan Stockman**

Right: First Great Western 57605 *Totnes Castle* passes Brea between Camborne and Redruth on 8 April 2014 with the 5Z11 Penzance T&RSMD–Plymouth driver training run. This was the first of a series of training runs in preparation for the launch of summer Saturday loco-hauled services on 31 May 2014. **Keith Barrow**

Published by Platform 5 Publishing Ltd, 52 Broadfield Road, Sheffield, S8 0XJ. England.

Printed in England by The Amadeus Press, Cleckheaton, West Yorkshire
ISBN: 978 1915984 16 6

❙ CONTENTS

THE CORNISH MAIN LINE AND ITS CONNECTIONS

Key

Closed Lines
Heritage lines
Freight-only lines
○ Open stations
○ Closed stations

North

Scale (miles)

0   5   10   15   20

© 2024 Platform 5 Publishing Ltd. Not all features shown.

INTRODUCTION

Change is a constant presence on the railway. Often change is subtle, but there are also periods of upheaval. Over the decades the railways of Cornwall have been shaped by the abolition of broad gauge, replacement of timber viaducts, nationalisation, the transition from steam to diesel-hydraulic and then diesel-electric traction, the Beeching closures, rationalisation of infrastructure, the introduction of HSTs, the switch from vacuum- to air-braked freight stock and the abolition of wagonload operations, Sprinterisation and privatisation.

The period between 2013 and 2023 was a time of transition and, in many ways, progress. This was a decade of investment, renewal and growth on Cornwall's railways, notable for the introduction of much more frequent services on the Cornish Main Line, the replacement of the HSTs with the new Hitachi-built Intercity Express Trains (IETs) and the modernisation of infrastructure. Passenger numbers grew steadily through the 1990s and 2000s, but Cornwall had continued to make do with essentially an hourly service linking the main towns and holiday hotspots in a region where tourism accounts for a significant share of the economy. Investment in signalling and the expansion of the GWR rolling stock fleet effectively enabled a half-hourly service with longer trains, finally giving the Cornish Main Line the service it needed.

Unfortunately, growth in passenger numbers came to an abrupt halt due to Covid-19 and in the wake of the pandemic train operators came under intense pressure from the government to cut costs. For GWR, this meant the premature withdrawal of the fleet of "Castle" HST sets, refurbished just a few years earlier to meet the latest accessibility standards. On the positive side, however, the government has allocated funding for the Mid-Cornwall Metro project, which will provide direct services between Newquay, Par, St Austell, Truro and Falmouth and passenger numbers are returning to pre-pandemic levels with strong growth in leisure travel.

At the start of the period covered by this book British Rail era rolling stock still dominated passenger operations in Cornwall, 16 years after privatisation. The only notable exception was the *Voyager* units used on the handful of CrossCountry services that extended west of the Tamar. On the freight side too, the 25-year-old four-wheel CDA hoppers introduced by BR continued to move china clay from the pits north of St Austell to the export terminal at Carne Point on the freight-only remnant of the scenic Lostwithiel–Fowey branch. However, modern traction in the form of the EMD-built Class 66s had taken over china clay workings from 1999, their improved haulage capabilities enabling the operation of longer (and therefore fewer) trains.

In 2010 I purchased my first DSLR camera and began making expeditions across Cornwall, recording the local railway scene among the varied landscapes of the peninsula. The challenge of photographing the unique china clay operations has provided much of the appeal for the hobby. However, with only one or two trains a day, capturing these workings often requires a combination of planning, patience and luck, particularly as the trains almost invariably run early, often hours ahead of schedule. On more than one occasion I made the 33-mile drive from my home to Lostwithiel under cloudless skies, only to find the Fowey valley shrouded in thick fog. Many times I returned home without the desired shot, but this only added the thrill of success when it eventually came.

Failure to obtain a clay shot was by no means a day wasted – the abundance of scenic locations in Cornwall meant there were always other options for photography. First Great Western's colourful "Dynamic Lines" and "Local Lines" always stood out in the lush green Cornish landscape. Furthermore, during the first half of the period covered by this book there were various one-off liveries on the HST and DMU fleets, which helped to add variety. By contrast, the all-pervasive dark green GWR livery that superseded the FGW schemes and spread across the fleet from 2015 onwards almost camouflages the trains in summer and is more of a challenge to photograph, although it can still look striking in favourable lighting conditions.

Alongside regular freight and passenger services, engineering trains, infrastructure measurement trains and charters have brought a variety of traction to the Cornish Main Line, while the return of daytime loco-hauled passenger workings using Class 57s and seated Mk 3 stock from the *Night Riviera Sleeper* on summer Saturdays provided a welcome boost for railway photography. This book illustrates some of the more unusual workings on the route over the last decade, alongside everyday scenes, many of which are already history.

Mechanical signalling with lower quadrant semaphores is a characteristic feature of Cornwall's railways and will remain so for the foreseeable future at a handful of locations despite the Mid-Cornwall Resignalling Programme (see Chapter 1), which will result in the closure of three signal boxes by March 2024. Signalling is therefore a focus throughout the book.

As in other parts of the UK, some of the photo locations featured in this book are no longer available due to lineside tree growth and other changes around the railway. However, elsewhere, vegetation clearance by Network Rail has opened up long-lost views. As a result of this long-term pattern of growth and clearance, the range of usable locations is in constant flux. To provide more options, in 2014 I obtained a 16 ft camera pole, with a Camranger device providing a Wi-Fi link between the camera and a smartphone. Two of the contributors to this book have used drones to obtain a completely different perspective on the railway and its place in the landscape.

On our journey westwards from the Tamar to Mount's Bay we will briefly consider the development of the Cornish Main Line and its heritage, but this book is not intended as a history of the route – for more background, I recommend the works of John Vaughan, in particular his *Illustrated History of the Cornish Main Line* (OPC, 2009). However, it does aim to provide an account of the changes in rolling stock, infrastructure and operations that have occurred between 2013 and 2023. Cornwall's branch lines and heritage railways will be covered in a separate book to be published by Platform 5 in the near future.

This book was only possible with the support of fellow photographers. I would like to thank Craig Munday, Nathan Stockman and Finbarr O'Neill for allowing the use of their wonderful images for this book, and for their company over many happy hours through rain and shine at the lineside in Cornwall.

Keith Barrow
Redruth, January 2024

CHAPTER 1: TEN YEARS OF CHANGE

This chapter explores the changes that took place between 2013 and 2023; the introduction of Intercity Express Trains (IETs) on services from London (and subsequently regional services from Bristol and South Wales), the transition from First Great Western's vibrant blue and pink livery to the rather more restrained GWR green, signalling enhancements enabling the launch of half-hourly services, and fluctuations in freight activities with traffic gained and lost.

Rolling stock changes

At the start of the period covered by this book First Great Western was by far the largest operator of HSTs, with well over 100 power cars, which had been re-engined with MTU power units in the 2000s. The first phase of the replacement of these trains had been on the cards for some time under the Department for Transport's Intercity Express Programme (IEP) but it would take until the end of the decade to oust the HSTs from their front-line duties and a residual HST fleet would be retained for regional services in the South-West well into the 2020s.

Replacement of the HSTs on services from London to Devon and Cornwall was not included in the IEP, which focussed on the procurement of new Class 800/801 Intercity Express Trains (IETs) for services from London to Bristol and South Wales, plus the East Coast Main Line. However, with the extension of electrification to Reading and Newbury, the HSTs showing their age and the advantages of operating a standardised fleet of modern trains with improved performance, lower emissions and greatly increased capacity, it was clear another order would come sooner rather than later.

In mid-2015 First Great Western (rebranded GWR from September 2015) announced that it had arranged the procurement of 173 additional IET vehicles through leasing company Eversholt to replace HSTs on services from London to Devon and Cornwall. The order initially comprised 22 5-car and seven 9-car bi-mode (diesel/25 kV AC electric) units, but this was subsequently increased with a further seven 9-car sets. The Class 802s are technically very similar to the Class 800s but feature modifications to the roof-mounted brake resistors for frequent operation along the seawall at Dawlish. Unlike the Class 800s and 801s, all except the first three Class 802s were assembled at Hitachi's plant at Pistoia in Italy because the company's new purpose-built plant at Newton Aycliffe in County Durham was operating at capacity supplying trains procured through the IEP. The GWR IET fleet therefore comprises vehicles assembled in three different countries, the first Class 800 and 802 sets having been built at Kasado in Japan.

By running under electric power between Paddington and Newbury, and with better acceleration than the HSTs, the introduction of the IETs reduced the fastest London–Penzance journey time by 14 minutes to 5h05. They have also significantly increased capacity – a 9-car Class 802/1 set seats 647 passengers, while two 5-car Class 802/0 sets (which often operate in multiple on Paddington–Penzance services) seat 652 – 24% more seats than an eight-car HST. To facilitate the introduction of the new trains

Above: With new equipment installed as part of the Mid-Cornwall Resignalling Programme visible in the bottom left of the picture, 802 003 approaches Par with 2C26, the 13.42 Plymouth–Penzance on 15 August 2023. IET units began to appear on Plymouth–Penzance and Cardiff–Penzance services following the decision to phase out the GWR HST fleet in 2022. *Keith Barrow*

Network Rail carried out gauge enhancement works between Plymouth and Penzance to accommodate the IET vehicles, which, at 26 m, were 3 m longer than the Mark 3 coaches they replaced.

The first IET sets to reach Cornwall were 800 003 and 800 004, which made a test run from Hitachi's North Pole depot in West London to Penzance on 22 June 2017. GWR began introducing the Class 800s on services out of Paddington from October 2017 – the cascade of 54 HST power cars to ScotRail had already commenced the previous month. The introduction of the Class 802s was swifter, with the first units entering service on 18 August 2018. Two days later 802 006 and 802 007 became the first of the class to be used in scheduled passenger service in Cornwall. The transition to the new fleet was completed on Saturday 18 May 2019, when crowds of enthusiasts lined the platforms at Paddington to witness the final HST workings out of Brunel's London terminus. The last HST from London to Cornwall had departed with considerably less fanfare the previous evening, when set OC45 worked the 17.03 Paddington–Penzance. The final Penzance–Paddington HST was the 06.50 from the Cornish terminus on 18 May.

The introduction of the IETs was not the end of GWR HSTs, however, and the operator retained a fleet of shortened sets to operate alongside DMUs on regional services in South-West England and South Wales, providing additional capacity and improved comfort. These have been dubbed "Castle Class" by GWR, a nod to the Great Western Railway Castle Class 4-6-0 steam locos associated with the West Country between the 1920s and the 1960s.

Initially the Castle fleet comprised 12 sets, each formed of two power cars and four Standard Class Mark 3s, which were upgraded by Wabtec in Doncaster with retention tank toilets and power-operated doors. Delays to the modification programme meant shortened sets of slam door Mark 3s were used on an interim basis until the end of 2019. GWR later acquired extra vehicles to form four more Castle sets. 36 power cars were retained, most being named after castles in South-West England and South Wales, and these were modified to operate power doors on the trailers. The main routes for the Castles were Taunton–Cardiff, Penzance–Cardiff and Penzance–Plymouth.

Following the Covid-19 pandemic train operators came under pressure from the government to cut spending and in late 2022 GWR issued an internal memo confirming it would withdraw the Castle fleet by the end of 2023 to reduce operating costs and emissions.

The rundown of the Castle fleet began in December 2022, when only ten sets were required (two for maintenance and eight in traffic), the remaining duties being taken over by IETs. Power car withdrawals began soon after with Class 43s being stopped as they became due for major exams. By May 2023 the active Castle fleet was down to 28 power cars and 12 Mark 3 sets covering eight diagrams. However, in April 2023 GWR announced it would retain some HSTs into 2024 to cover for DMUs undergoing overhaul.

With the withdrawal of the Castle fleet and the CrossCountry HSTs Plymouth Laira depot has taken over most maintenance of

the Class 802s from Stoke Gifford depot near Bristol Parkway and North Pole depot in West London.

Disposal of the surplus Castle sets began in summer 2023 and after being stripped for spares 43005, 43041 and 43171 were the first power cars to go for scrap, being moved by road from Laira to Sims Metals at Newport Docks in early July. In early August 43022, 43158 and 43170, together with six ex-LNER Mark 3s and one former East Midlands Railway vehicle, were shipped from Great Yarmouth to Mexico.

From 10 September 2023 the Castles were reduced to just three daily diagrams and several more sets were taken out of traffic, two of which briefly went into warm store on the West Somerset Railway. In November 2023 six former Castle power cars (43009/010/016/040/172/192) together with five ex-CrossCountry power cars and 11 trailers from the Castle fleet were exported to Nigeria. Further exports to Mexico and Nigeria were expected in early 2024. From December 2023 the three remaining Castle diagrams were concentrated on Plymouth–Penzance (with one extended back to Exeter St Davids), making the Cornish Main Line the last bastion of regular HST operation in England. 19 power cars remained in the GWR fleet in December 2023 – 43004/027/029/042/092–094/097/098/122/153–156/186–189/198.

Night Riviera Sleeper

The only regular loco-hauled passenger train in Cornwall is the *Night Riviera Sleeper* between Paddington and Penzance, which runs every night except Saturday, operated by GWR using its fleet of four Class 57/6 locos (57602–605) introduced in 2004 and Mark 3 stock, which has been used on these services since 1983. During the period under review an extra loco was often hired from another operator, usually Direct Rail Services, to bolster the fleet.

The coaches were extensively refurbished in 2017/18 at a cost of £14 million, and the first internally refurbished day coach was delivered to GWR in September 2016. Both the Class 57s and the sleeper stock were transferred from Old Oak Common to Penzance depot in 2019 (see "depot expansion" section below).

With a shortage of DMUs, First Great Western took the welcome decision in 2014 to use a Class 57 and the Mark 3 seated stock from the sleeper to operate Summer Saturday regional services on the main line through Devon and Cornwall, releasing a DMU to strengthen services elsewhere. This continued to run each summer until 2018, the internal cascade of DMUs and the introduction of the Castle HST sets ensuring the Class 57s would no longer be required for daytime operations.

DMU changes

Increasing passenger numbers meant that by 2013 the First Great Western DMU fleet was under strain. Many regional services on

Right: From 2019 many of the HST power cars retained by GWR as part of the "Castle Class" fleet were named after castles in South West England and South Wales, receiving attractive cast nameplates as shown on 43042 *Tregenna Castle*. **Joshua Barrow**

the Cornish Main Line were in the hands of 2-car Class 150 and single-car Class 153 units, the latter usually operating in pairs or with a Class 150. In 2010/11 FGW inherited Class 150/1 units from London Overground and London Midland, which had been cascaded to the West Country following the introduction of new Class 172 *Turbostar* DMUs in the London and Birmingham areas respectively. The 150/1s operated alongside FGW's Class 150/2 units, most of which were from the former Wessex Trains franchise. Class 158s became extremely scarce in Cornwall from the late 2000s as the FGW units were largely concentrated on the Cardiff–Portsmouth route and services in the Bristol area.

With the electrification of the Great Western Main Line, Thames Valley suburban services were taken over by Class 387 *Electrostar* EMUs from September 2016 onwards, enabling the transfer of Class 166 DMUs to Bristol St Philip's Marsh depot from summer 2017. This in turn allowed the cascading of Class 150/2s and Class 158s from the Bristol area to duties further west. In Cornwall this resulted in Class 150/2s working most branch services and the Class 158s largely operating on the main line. This allowed GWR to dispense with its Class 150/0, 150/1 and 153 units; the withdrawal of the latter spelt the end of single-car DMU operation in Cornwall in March 2019.

CrossCountry

The operation of CrossCountry (XC) services in Cornwall saw few changes in the period under review. Services to Newquay have not run since the Covid-19 pandemic but the service from Penzance to Scotland was increased from one to two trains per day in each direction from May 2023. The Aberdeen–Penzance service is the longest on the UK network with a scheduled journey time of 13h15 for the 785-mile trip.

Between 2013 and 2023 most XC services in Cornwall remained in the hands of the Class 220 *Voyager* and Class 221 *Super Voyager* units that replaced HSTs and Class 47-hauled trains on South West–North East services in 2002. XC's small fleet of HSTs continued to reach Newquay and Penzance on summer Saturdays until 2019, after which there were no booked XC HST workings west of Plymouth. However, prior to their withdrawal in September 2023 the XC HSTs still occasionally reached Penzance, deputising for an unavailable *Voyager*. The final XC HST working in Cornwall occurred on 9 May 2023, when 43239 and InterCity "Executive" liveried 43184 worked 1Z58 16.45 Bristol Temple Meads–Penzance and 2C80 22.08 Penzance–Plymouth in place of the usual *Voyager* due to flooding in the Bristol area.

Depot expansion

In 2017 work began on a £22 million project to expand the depot at Long Rock (Penzance T&RSMD) and improve maintenance facilities, enabling the depot to handle an increased workload. The project was completed in 2019, when the *Night Riviera* Class 57s and sleeper stock were transferred to Penzance from Old Oak Common HST depot, which closed to make way for High Speed 2.

In April 2022 Network Rail and GWR started work on a £6.5 million project to construct three new sidings at Ponsandane west of Long Rock depot and around a mile from Penzance station to stable and service 9- and 10-car IET trains. The project is due to be completed in 2024.

GWR revival

A notable change in the appearance of the railway in Cornwall began in 2015, when First Great Western was renamed Great Western Railway (GWR). The GWR logo had first appeared in refurbished Mark 3 coaches in 2014 and a new dark green livery

with silver lining began to appear on rolling stock in summer 2015 with the company being officially rebranded GWR on 20 September 2015. The revival of the historical identity and the launch of the new livery coincided with the Great Western Route Modernisation and the introduction of the new IET train fleet. Despite their imminent replacement a few full-length HST sets were repainted in GWR livery, although the swapping of vehicles between sets soon resulted in mixed formations of old and new liveries. Within a few years the dark green livery had become pervasive, although two Class 150/2 DMUs still clung on to their faded FGW blue/pink paintwork at the end of 2023.

Infrastructure/signalling

Following the closure of much of Cornwall's railway network in the 1960s, rationalisation of the remaining routes continued through the 1970s and 1980s. Signalling block sections were lengthened to enable the closure of signal boxes and in October 1986 the eight-mile section between Burngullow and Probus was singled to reduce operating costs. While these decisions may have made financial sense to BR at the time, they were proving to be an increasing headache by the 2000s as passenger numbers began to increase and calls for more reliable and frequent services grew louder. The stretch of single track became a serious bottleneck, particularly when trains were already running late, and the down line was reinstated by Network Rail on 21 November 2004 at a cost of £14 million.

The signalling problem remained however, with block sections as long as 14 miles, which hampered the recovery from delays. Furthermore, aspirations to increase frequencies on the Cornish Main Line from one to two trains per hour (see below) could only be realised with improved signalling.

In 2016 the cost of completely resignalling the main line through West Devon and Cornwall was estimated at £200 million. This was deemed too costly but £60 million was made available for additional intermediate block sections to enable more frequent services, plus the modernisation of level crossings. A £30 million scheme to add 21 additional signals and upgrade seven level crossings was jointly funded by the Department for Transport through Network Rail, Cornwall Council, Cornwall and Isles of Scilly Local Enterprise Partnership and the EU's European Structural and Investment Funds Growth Programme 2014–2020.

An additional block section installed at Menheniot is controlled from the Plymouth panel. Bodmin Parkway gained two extra stop signals, one on each line with a banner repeater on the down main, while track circuits were replaced with axle counters. At the time of writing these are controlled from Lostwithiel signal box, where a new panel was installed. Roskear signal box near Camborne also gained a new panel controlling new signals installed to break up a 14-mile section that had existed since BR rationalised signalling between Truro and Redruth in the 1980s.

A further £40 million was later allocated to enable the resignalling of the Blachford–Plymouth and Lostwithiel–Truro sections. The Mid-Cornwall Resignalling Programme will result in the closure of Lostwithiel, Par and Truro signal boxes and the elimination of semaphore signalling at these locations, with control of these areas plus the intermediate block sections at St Austell, Burngullow and Probus passing to a workstation at Exeter signalling centre. This means the stretch from west of Liskeard to Chacewater, the short stretch of the Par–Newquay branch as far as St Blazey and the freight-only Fowey and Parkandillack branches will be controlled from Devon.

The work, which was carried out by Siemens, was due to be completed by November 2023, but at the time of writing had been delayed to March 2024. Signal boxes will remain in operation at Liskeard, Roskear (Camborne), St Erth and Penzance and

Above: GWR 43042 *Tregenna Castle* passes Penstraze between Redruth and Truro leading 2U20, the 10.50 Penzance–Cardiff, and begins the long 1 in 80 descent to Penwithers Junction on 17 May 2023. On the left in front of the bridge is one of the additional signals installed in 2018 to reduce the length of block sections, enabling the introduction of half-hourly passenger services on the Cornish Main Line. *Keith Barrow*

A scene little changed in over a century: sunrise at St Erth signal box on 15 October 2022. *Craig Munday*

semaphore signals will be retained at Liskeard and St Erth. The programme includes very few changes to track layouts. At Truro the trailing crossover at the eastern end of the station will be replaced with a facing crossover, enabling bidirectional operation through the up main platform, while trap points in the bay and off the Falmouth branch will be abolished. At Par the down loop will be redesignated a passenger loop.

Track remodelling saw the removal of redundant sidings at St Erth, St Austell and Lostwithiel during the period covered by this book. Hayle viaduct underwent a £7 million renovation, which involved closure of the line for 16 days in November 2014 to enable complete replacement of around 1000 deck timbers and 4500 rivets as well as corrosion repairs.

There have also been improvements at stations. The £10 million St Erth Mutimodal Hub project, which was 54%-funded by the EU, involved building a 422-space car park south of the station and expanding the existing car park, with improved access to the A30 trunk road. This has enabled St Erth to take over from Lelant Saltings as the Park and Ride station for the busy St Ives branch, removing traffic from the local road network in Lelant. The new Park and Ride facilities opened in May 2019. Construction began in early 2023 on a new wheelchair-accessible footbridge, which will be equipped with two lifts.

New lounges for First Class and *Night Riviera Sleeper* passengers were built at Penzance and Truro stations and passenger Wi-Fi was installed at all stations in Cornwall.

Service improvements

Passenger numbers on the Cornish Main Line reached 4.5 million in 2018, having doubled in 20 years, yet frequencies had remained largely unchanged with a roughly hourly service between Penzance and Plymouth. The introduction of half-hourly services on the Truro–Falmouth branch in 2009 demonstrated what was possible – passenger numbers at Falmouth Docks station increased by 266% between 2002 and 2010, while Penryn saw growth of 247% over this period.

For many years there had been aspirations for two trains per hour in each direction on the main line and this was finally made possible by the resignalling work outlined above. This enabled the operation of two trains per hour from December 2018 and from 20 May 2019 seven extra services were added in each direction between Plymouth and Penzance, increasing weekday capacity by 4000 seats, with the full half-hourly service commencing in December 2019, when Penzance–London journey times were also cut by 14 minutes thanks to timetable changes on the Berks & Hants route.

These improvements helped to fuel continued growth in passenger numbers. The total number of entries and exits through Cornwall's stations reached 6.4 million in 2019–20, and although traffic plunged during the Covid-19 pandemic, with the figure dropping to just 2.4 million in 2020/21, by 2023 passenger numbers were gradually returning to pre-pandemic levels with a stronger recovery in the leisure sector.

In January 2023 Cornwall Council received a £50 million government grant to fund the £56.8 million Mid Cornwall Metro project, which will enable direct services linking four of Cornwall's largest urban areas (Newquay, St Austell, Truro, and Falmouth/Penryn). Most of the enhancements will take place on the Newquay branch, providing capacity for more frequent services. The introduction of the through Newquay–Falmouth service will provide three trains per hour on the section of the Cornish Main Line between Par, St Austell and Truro.

Below: 150 123 climbs away from Lostwithiel with 2C47, the 13.49 Plymouth–Penzance on 4 October 2015. Following electrification in the Thames Valley and the subsequent cascade of Class 166 DMUs to the South-West GWR dispensed with its Class 150/0 and 150/1 units, with 150 123 joining the Northern fleet. In Spring 2023 the GWR Class 150 fleet comprised 20 Class 150/2 units allocated to Exeter depot and primarily used on branch services in Devon and Cornwall. *Keith Barrow*

Above: With just a few weeks remaining before the withdrawal of the last regular freight working on the Cornish Main Line west of Burngullow Junction, 66176 passes Trenowth between Truro and St Austell with the weekly Penzance T&RSMD–St Blazey empty fuel tanks on 13 October 2013. *Nathan Stockman*

Freight

Despite a significant decline in volumes in recent decades, china clay continues to dominate rail freight operations in Cornwall, with DB Cargo moving the commodity in two distinct types of operation.

A weekly train conveys Cornish china clay to the Cliffe Vale terminal near Stoke-on-Trent using bogie JIA wagons, 26 of which were ordered for clay producer Imerys by wagon company NACCO in 2000 and built by Arbel Fauvet in France. The 90 tonne wagons, which have a payload of 63 tonnes, entered service in 2001. The train runs from Parkandillack/Treviscoe (north of St Austell on

the freight-only branch from Burngullow Junction) to St Blazey, where wagons from Par Docks are often added to the train, before continuing to Exeter Riverside yard. From here the train runs to Bescot yard and then to Cliffe Vale. The transport of bagged clay in Cargowaggon bogie vans ended in 2013 and all traffic is now in bulk form.

Export china clay is conveyed from the loading points at Parkandillack and Treviscoe, and from Goonbarrow Junction (Rocks Dryers) near Bugle on the Par–Newquay branch to the export terminal at Fowey Dock Carne Point. Due to the gradients on the Parkandillack branch trains are sometimes worked to

Right: China clay and GWR lower quadrant semaphores have both been synonymous with Cornwall's railways since the 19th century. On 16 May 2016 another trainload of clay makes its way through Lostwithiel bound for export via the Carne Point terminal at Fowey. The four-wheel CDA clay hoppers were withdrawn in August 2023 and the semaphores at Lostwithiel were due to disappear in November 2023, although delays to the resignalling programme have ensured their survival into 2024. *Keith Barrow*

Burngullow in two portions. A reversal is required at Lostwithiel for trains to access the scenic freight-only branch to Carne Point, the remnant of the former line to Fowey, which lost its passenger service in 1965.

Until summer 2023 export china clay was conveyed in 29 tonne-capacity two-axle CDA hopper wagons, derived from the once ubiquitous HAA merry-go-round coal hoppers. Following the conversion of a prototype from a HAA, which remained in Cornwall as part of the CDA fleet, 124 of these wagons were built at Doncaster Works in 1987/88 to replace the distinctive OOV "Clay Hood" wagons. A further 14 CDAs were rebuilt from HAA hoppers by RFS at Doncaster in 1989.

For many years it was common to see short trains of clay hoods, and later CDAs, running to Fowey from various loading points each day. Trains would run to Lostwithiel and wagons would then be tripped down the 4.5 mile branch between Lostwithiel and the export terminal at Fowey Carne Point, usually by a different loco. When the CDAs were introduced in the late 1980s one loco was diagrammed to make up to eight return trips per day along the Fowey branch, the train plan varied from week-to-week, depending on the requirements of the clay producers.

However, with the number of loading points in decline, the practice of tripping wagons from Lostwithiel to Fowey ended, with trains running direct from their origin to the port. The yard at Lostwithiel fell into disuse, although trains to and from Fowey continue to use the loops here for the loco to run round.

Changes in the china clay industry and the streamlining of rail operations have resulted in a much leaner and more efficient

method of working. Today just one Class 66 is required for these weekday-only workings and usually only one train a day runs to Carne Point from either Parkandillack/Treviscoe (usually the latter) or Goonbarrow Junction. In 2008 the maximum train length was increased from 32 to 38 CDAs with a total payload of 1140 tonnes.

With the decline in volumes fewer CDAs were required for the residual clay flows. Many CDAs were stored at St Blazey yard and before being scrapped, early withdrawals including the prototype and the batch of wagons converted from HAAs. Trials with bogie JIA wagons took place on the Fowey branch in April 2023 and these proved to be a success. To supplement the fleet of JIAs five JGA covered aggregate hoppers formerly used on trains from the Tarmac quarry at Rylstone in North Yorkshire were resurrected from store for use on trains to Fowey, although at the time of writing it is unclear whether these vehicles will be suitable for this purpose and all clay traffic to Fowey was being conveyed in JIAs in early 2024. The era of four-wheel wagons on china clay trains in Cornwall ended on 11 August 2023, and following the final revenue CDA working from Treviscoe to Carne Point the remaining CDAs congregated at St Blazey yard to await their fate. Scrapping began the following month and by early 2024 most of the CDAs had been cut up at St Blazey. Happily, however, nine CDAs were secured for preservation in late 2023; eight acquired by the National Wagon Preservation Group will remain in Cornwall at the Bodmin & Wenford Railway, while one purchased by the CDA 375 030 Preservation Group is now based at the Plym Valley Railway.

Below: Mid-July 2023 saw a trial flow of sand from Methrose Siding at Burngullow to Longport for Land Recovery Ltd. The trains, which were operated by Colas Rail, arrived as one set of 20 almost new JNA-V wagons and left in two portions to Exeter. On 20 July 2023, the second day of loading, 70811 extracts the second portion of the train from Methrose Siding before running around and heading to Exeter as 6Z58 18.00 Burngullow Junction–Exeter Riverside. *Nathan Stockman*

China clay trains are exclusively worked by DB Cargo Class 66 locos based at St Blazey depot, where the wagons are also maintained. Loco swaps are generally performed by means of the long-haul flow from Cliffe Vale, but the "local" Class 66 can sometimes remain in Cornwall for many weeks. The china clay branches and St Blazey depot and yard will be covered in Part 2 of this book.

China clay production generates large quantities of waste material. The coarser material can be used in various forms of construction as aggregate, but the remoteness of the clay operations from major centres of population has long been a barrier to its wider use. However, such secondary aggregates are exempt from an environmental tax on primary aggregates dug from the ground, which was introduced in 2002, and this has helped to make mineral waste from Cornwall's china clay pits more attractive to the construction industry. The result has been sporadic flows of sand from Cornwall to the London area. In 2007 Freightliner began operating sand trains from Methrose Siding at the eastern end of the Burngullow ECC complex conveying material for use at the site of the 2012 Olympic Games at Stratford.

Traffic resumed in 2013/14, when DB Schenker and Mendip Rail operated trains from the same location conveying sand destined for Bow East yard in east London. Two trial trains ran in June 2015 as part of proposals to expand Bow East as a major hub for building materials in the capital, but the scheme failed to gain planning consent.

In autumn 2018 two further Burngullow–Bow trial trains ran conveying aggregate for use in the production of concrete blocks. This proved successful and a regular train began running in November 2018. The train, which operated until Autumn 2019, ran in two portions between Burngullow and Exeter Riverside, where it was combined before running overnight to Bow East.

The traffic returned once more in July 2023, again on a trial basis, this time operated by Colas Rail with trains running to Longport in Staffordshire and hauled by Class 70 locomotives.

The development of lithium mining could offer further grounds for optimism for the future of rail freight in Cornwall. In 2023 Imerys acquired an 80% stake in British Lithium, which is planning to produce battery-grade lithium carbonate from Cornish granite. Inferred mineral resources are estimated at 161 million tonnes at a grade of 0.54% lithium oxide and a mine could operate for more than 30 years at a production rate of 20 000 tonnes of lithium carbonate equivalent annually.

A notable freight development during the period covered by this book was the resumption of cement traffic to Moorswater near Liskeard, which brought freight trains back to the northern end of the Looe branch. Trains ran to the former English China Clays facility at Moorswater adjacent to the A38 in the shadow of Moorswater viaduct. Clay traffic to the works ceased in 1997 but in 1999 Blue Circle opened a cement depot on the site of the clay dryers. This saw the reopening of the short section of line from Coombe Junction to Moorswater, which received cement in liquid and bagged form from Hope in Derbyshire and Westbury in Wiltshire. Trains were operated by EWS (now DB Cargo) and Freightliner but traffic ceased in 2013.

However, with the reopening of the rail terminal at Aberthaw cement works in South Wales in 2016 the stage was set for the revival of Cornish cement traffic. Following a gauging run with 70809 in June the first train of cement from Aberthaw arrived at Moorswater on 30 November 2016 behind 70808. The train was operated by Colas Rail and ran weekly using four-wheel PCA tank wagons. The lack of an east-facing connection between the Cornish Main Line and the Looe branch at Liskeard complicated operations and due to the length of the train the loco usually ran round at Lostwithiel, bringing an extra freight working through the Glynn valley, although on a few occasions the loco ran round at Liskeard. This meant the Aberthaw–Moorswater train was booked to cross both Liskeard and Moorswater viaducts (the latter twice), before passing beneath both structures again on the final leg of its journey to Moorswater.

Traction was usually a Class 70, although Colas Rail Class 66s worked the train on a few occasions. Sadly, the revival was brief and after just under four years traffic ceased once more. The final train ran on 25 November 2020 after Tarmac ended rail operations at Aberthaw, with the Tarmac cement distribution depot at Moorswater closing the following month.

Fuel was delivered to Long Rock depot (Penzance T&RSMD) and other depots in the South-West by rail for many years, originating from Fawley refinery in Hampshire. From 2008 this operated as a weekly train with portions for the First Great Western depots at Bristol St Phillips Marsh, Plymouth Laira and Long Rock. At Tavistock Junction yard in Plymouth the train was split into portions for Laira and Long Rock, the latter being tripped to St Blazey and thence to Penzance.

The final rail delivery of fuel to Long Rock took place on 25 October 2013 and the seven empty TTA tanks were collected by 66075 on 8 November, bringing the curtain down on scheduled freight operations on the Cornish Main Line west of Burngullow Junction. Gas oil traffic continued to run to St Blazey for a few more months but this also ceased in early 2014. This was the last rail-borne petroleum traffic in Devon and Cornwall.

In 2005 scrap merchant Henry Orchards & Sons of St Austell began dispatching scrap metal by rail to South Wales. The train was operated by EWS (rebranded DB Schenker from January 2009 and now DB Cargo), generally using a pool of five MBA "Monster Box" bogie open wagons, which were loaded at St Blazey yard and destined for Cardiff Tidal yard. Loaded wagons were generally dispatched from St Blazey fortnightly (sometimes more frequently) and were often combined with other traffics such as empty fuel wagons from Long Rock depot and china clay. However, with the loss of these flows the scrap traffic became uneconomic to operate and ceased in January 2014.

Chapter 2: Saltash–Liskeard

The main line makes a dramatic entrance into Cornwall, Isambard Kingdom Brunel's iconic Royal Albert Bridge carrying the railway high above the tidal waters of the River Tamar, which forms the border between Devon and Cornwall. The 2188 ft-long bridge comprises two lenticular iron trusses, each 455 ft long, with plate girder approach spans.

The Lower Tamar Valley was a formidable natural barrier that would require both engineering ingenuity and a significant financial commitment to overcome. At Saltash the river is 1100 ft wide and 80 ft deep. To complicate matters further, the Admiralty, which was responsible for navigable waterways, insisted that the structure provide clearance of at least 100 ft above the high-water mark.

Brunel's initial designs for a timber viaduct were rejected by the Admiralty, which insisted on a single pier in the navigable part of the river. The great engineer's solution was a bridge comprising 10 masonry piers on the Cornish side and seven in Devon with two arched wrought iron trusses carried in mid-stream by a single cast iron pier, providing the necessary 100 ft vertical clearance. This was approved by the Admiralty and construction began in 1854.

Due to the depth of the bedrock, it was necessary to sink a long metal tube below the water and mud to find a firm foundation for the central pier. Water was then pumped out of the cylinder to enable construction. However, the project was soon hit by soaring costs and the bankruptcy of the contractor. This prompted Brunel to take over project management and to save money the bridge was redesigned with a single track. The bridge's two main spans were assembled on the shore, floated into position, then jacked up by a few feet per day to reach the required height. The first of the main

elliptical trusses was positioned in July 1858 and the second in March 1859.

The bridge was inaugurated by Prince Albert on 2 May 1859, although sadly Brunel was unable to attend the opening ceremony for his masterpiece due to ill health and he died on 5 September that year. Following his death the legend "I.K. BRUNEL – ENGINEER – 1859" was placed above both portals of the central spans as a tribute. By the early 1950s the lettering had been partly obscured behind an ugly maintenance walkway but this was removed in 2007 to mark the 200th anniversary of Brunel's birth.

With the increasing weight of trains the bridge was strengthened several times in the 20th Century and the approach spans were replaced in the 1930s. Major renovation took place in 1969, when further strengthening work was carried out with installation of additional horizontal bracing. In 2009 Network Rail refurbished the two main spans, with contractors stripping off 30 layers of paintwork to bare metal before applying a grey epoxy glass-flake paint, which is intended to provide 25 years of maintenance-free anti-corrosion protection.

The line reverts to double track as it enters Saltash station, 250 miles 8 chains from London Paddington via Bristol Temple Meads and Plymouth Millbay. The station building on the up platform at Saltash was derelict for many years until it was purchased by Saltash Town Council in 2017. The building has

Above: 43040 *Berry Pomeroy Castle* leads 2C27, the 14.18 Plymouth–Penzance service across the Royal Albert Bridge into Cornwall and Saltash station on 25 May 2023. More than a century separates the railway bridge, inaugurated on 2 May 1859, and the road bridge, opened on 26 April 1962. ***Keith Barrow***

Left: 43165 *Prince Michael of Kent* leads 1C47, the 10.03 Paddington–Penzance across the Royal Albert Bridge into Saltash on 15 March 2018. ***Finbarr O'Neill***

Above: At low tide DB Cargo 66165 crosses the 86 ft high Coombe by Saltash Viaduct with the 6C53 Parkandillack–Exeter Riverside china clay on 25 May 2023. Like many viaducts on the Cornish Main Line this is a replacement for an earlier timber structure and was completed in 1894. *Keith Barrow*

Above: DB Cargo 66034 passes Wearde near Saltash with 6W98, the 08.00 Truro–Eastleigh East Yard continuous welded rail train on 23 April 2017. The train is approaching the site of Defiance Platform, which closed in 1930. *Keith Barrow*

Above: Viaducts are a characteristic feature of the Saltash–St Germans section of the Cornish Main Line, carrying the railway across various tributaries of the River Tamar. The 08.40 Reading–Penzance GWR service passes Trematon Castle as it crosses Forder Viaduct on 23 April 2017. The 699 ft viaduct was built as part of the 1908 deviation between Defiance Platform and St Germans. The original wooden viaduct crossed the inlet in the foreground. This view was taken from Churchtown Farm Community Nature Reserve. **Keith Barrow**

Above: GB Railfreight 66732 *GBRf The First Decade 1999-2000 John Smith MD* and Colas Rail 66848 top-and-tail 6G98, the 14.27 Westbury–Burngullow continuous welded rail train across Forder Viaduct on 21 July 2021. In the background is the river Tamar and beyond it Devonport Dockyard. **Craig Munday**

Above: On summer Saturdays between 2014 and 2018 Class 57 locos and Mark 3 coaches normally used on *Night Riviera Sleeper* trains were pressed into daytime service, providing extra capacity (and comfort!) on the main line through Cornwall and Devon during the busy summer holiday period. On 6 September 2014, the final day of the 2014 season, hire-in 57305 crosses the River Lynher on the 618 ft Notter Viaduct with 2E75 , the 11.25 Par–Exeter St Davids. This was the only time a Network Rail-liveried Class 57 worked this train and the only appearance by a non-First Great Western Class 57 during the 2014 season. ***Nathan Stockman***

Above: The first HST set in GWR green with 43187 leading (and 43188 at the rear) is captured with the River Lynher and boatyard in the background on 29 September 2015, a few days after the new branding was officially launched. ***Nathan Stockman***

Above: Colas Rail 70811 crosses the 978 ft St Germans Viaduct with 6C35, the 22.30 Aberthaw–Moorswater cement tanks soon after high tide on an unseasonably warm 27 February 2019. This was usually a Class 70 duty but occasionally brought a Colas Rail Class 66 to Cornwall. Following the decline in freight on the Cornish Main Line in the 1990s and 2000s, the return of cement traffic to Moorswater in 2016 was a welcome boost for rail freight in Cornwall, but sadly this working was short lived with trains ceasing once more in November 2020. *Keith Barrow*

Above: 802 114 passes St Germans station with an afternoon Penzance–Paddington GWR service on 17 June 2022. The coach in the background is former London & South Western Railway luggage van 1353, which was built at Eastleigh in 1896. Following withdrawal in August 1932 the coach was used as accommodation at a site near Wadebridge, where it was discovered in 1995, derelict but largely complete. The vehicle was purchased by the owner of the station building, completely restored, including an external repaint in its original LSWR livery, and mounted on a replica chassis. 1353 is now used as holiday accommodation, along with 1889-built GWR travelling post office coach 846, which is located alongside the up platform at the other end of the station. *Keith Barrow*

Above: Days after participating in the final HST workings from London Paddington, the first production HST power car, 43002 *Sir Kenneth Grange* is relegated to regional service, appropriately paired with last-built power car 43198 as it approaches St Germans heading east on 22 May 2019. At this time work to upgrade GWR's "Castle Class" HST sets with power doors was running behind schedule and some short sets were formed with slam door Mark 3s to bridge the gap. 43198 was one of the power cars modified to operate with power door-equipped Mark 3s and was still in service with GWR as part of the "Castle" fleet at the end of 2023 but 43002 was withdrawn in 2019 and is now on display at the National Railway Museum in York. *Nathan Stockman*

since been restored to provide waiting facilities and toilets for passengers, as well as a community hall and business hub. The renovation was completed in November 2021.

Just south of Saltash station the line crosses Coombe by Saltash Viaduct, the first of many viaducts on the Cornish Main Line. Cornwall's topography is defined by deep north-south valleys and as the route generally runs east-west it must cross many of these valleys. The Cornish Main Line was constructed in the 1850s, a time of low market confidence in railway investment following the "Railway Mania" of the previous decade. As a result, the line between Saltash, Truro and Falmouth was built within a constrained budget, and viaducts were constructed with timber deck spans supported by fans of timber bracing built on masonry piers. The replacement of these structures with masonry viaducts began in the 1870s and the current Coombe by Saltash Viaduct was completed in 1894.

The line then passes the site of Defiance Platform, which was built by the Royal Navy in 1905 for the up to 1000 personnel based at HMS Defiance, although it was also open to the public. The first station was a single platform, which was replaced by two platforms just to the east of the original site when the new alignment to St Germans opened. Defiance Platform closed after just 25 years in October 1930.

The 1908 alignment to St Germans was built by the GWR to replace the Cornwall Railway's original 1859 single-track route, which ran closer to the River Tamar, crossing the tidal inlets on a series of wooden viaducts. Following closure, a section of the 1859 line remained in use at the Saltash end as a carriage siding until the 1960s. Interestingly, all mileposts west of St Germans still refer to the distance from London Paddington (via Plymouth Millbay and Bristol Temple Meads) via the original alignment, which was two chains longer than the deviation.

The first major structure on the 1908 line is the 699 ft Forder Viaduct, located just to the south of Trematon Castle, which is visible from the train. The line then passes through the 451 yd Shillingham Tunnel before crossing the River Lynher on the 618 ft Notter Viaduct. The 1859 alignment is crossed just to the east of St Germans Viaduct. At 978 ft this is the longest viaduct on the deviation, its 17 arches carrying the line up to 106 ft above the muddy estuary of the River Tiddy.

The line then curves to the north-west regaining the original 1859 alignment before entering the two-platform St Germans station. On the up platform the single storey Cornwall Railway station building, which is Grade II listed, survives as a private dwelling. A notable feature of this station is the 1889-built GWR travelling post office coach and 1896 London & South Western Railway luggage van alongside the up platform, which have been tastefully converted to holiday accommodation and restored to their 19th century liveries.

East of St Germans the line heads away from the Tamar estuary and immediately the gradients begin to steepen, with a 1 in

Above: GWR 158 798 climbs away from its stop at St Germans with 2C47, the 12.53 Exeter St Davids–Penzance on 6 April 2019. *Keith Barrow*

Above: Running 65 minutes late, 43198 *Driver Stan Martin/Driver Brian Cooper* leads 2C73, the 11.00 Cardiff Central–Penzance GWR service near Polbathic on the 1 in 68 climb towards Trerulefoot on 11 August 2022. 43040 is at the rear of the train. *Keith Barrow*

Above: Passengers on 1C99, the 23.50 Paddington–Penzance *Night Riviera Sleeper* awake to glorious views of the Cornish countryside as 57604 *Pendennis Castle* sweeps through the reverse curve at Trerulefoot between St Germans and Menheniot on 16 May 2016. ***Keith Barrow***

Above: Following the withdrawal of cement trains to Moorswater in 2020 the only regular freight traffic between Lostwithiel and Plymouth is the weekly flow of china clay from Treviscoe/Parkandillack to Cliffe Vale in the Potteries. This is operated by DB Cargo using JIA bogie hoppers owned by wagon leasing company Nacco and leased to china clay producer Imerys. PD Ports liveried 66109 *Teesport Express* (complete with Thornaby depot sticker above the right light cluster) passes Trerulefoot with 6C10, the 14.16 Burngullow ECC–Exeter Riverside on 15 June 2023. ***Keith Barrow***

78 climb out of the station followed by a 1 in 68 for westbound trains. The line winds through rolling countryside with excellent views north towards Bodmin Moor, crossing the 525 ft long, 93 ft high Tresulgan Viaduct, which dates from 1899 and replaced an earlier timber viaduct. A more notable structure is the 795 ft long, Coldrennick Viaduct. Rising 138 ft from the valley floor, this is the fifth highest viaduct on the Cornish Main Line. The current structure has 16 piers with iron girders and dates from 1898 when this section of the line was doubled. During reconstruction in February 1897 a working platform occupied by 17 men under the bridge deck broke away and fell 138 ft into the valley below, killing 12 men. With the increasing weight of trains, the piers of the viaduct were strengthened in 1933, when they were encased in stone.

The line then enters the two-platform Menheniot station. In 1964 British Railways announced the closure of seven stations on the Cornish Main Line and only Menheniot was reprieved. The station has been an unstaffed halt since 1965 and is more than a mile from the village of Menheniot. The station building on the down side was destroyed by fire but a waiting shelter survives on the up platform. In the next two-and-a-half miles the line crosses three viaducts: Treviddo (486 ft long, 101 ft high), Cartuther (411 ft long, 89 ft high) and Bolitho (546 ft long, 113 ft high). Just west of Bolitho Viaduct Liskeard's outer signal comes into view,

this lower quadrant being the most easterly semaphore signal on the Cornish Main Line.

The Liskeard–Looe branch is then crossed on the 720 ft long, 150 ft high Liskeard Viaduct. This was first rebuilt in 1894, when the brick piers were raised and iron girders were installed to replace the original timber upper structure. The iron girders were replaced with steel in 1929.

The line then passes Liskeard signal box and the west-facing connection from the up line to the Looe branch before entering Liskeard station. Crossovers at both ends of the station provide access to the Looe branch, although these are only used by empty passenger, freight, and engineering trains as there are no through services from the Looe branch to the main line.

Built in 1915 to replace a structure dating from 1892, Liskeard signal box is located at the eastern end of the down platform and has a 36-lever frame.

The two main line platforms are situated in a deep cutting and the Brunel-designed booking office, which was modernised in 2004, is at street level. A road bridge spans the cutting, and a footbridge connects the platforms at a lower level.

The Looe branch platform was a later addition to the station, dating from 1901, and is positioned at right angles to the main line with access via the up main line platform. The 1901 station building on the Looe platform still stands.

Below: Freightliner 66528 *Madge Elliot MBE* drops down the gradient past Budges Shop near Trerulefoot with a lengthy train of Network Rail MRA side-tipping ballast wagons on 26 February 2022. 66542 is at the rear of the train. Freightliner has no booked freight trains in Cornwall but the operator's Class 66 locos occasionally visit the Duchy on engineering trains. Rising to 1217 feet above sea level, Caradon Hill on Bodmin Moor is prominent on the horizon. *Craig Munday*

Above: Ripening maize fields and a dramatic sky provide an attractive backdrop for Regional Railways-liveried 37425 *Sir Robert McAlpine/Concrete Bob* at Bethany as the DRS-owned loco heads back to Devon on a route learning run from Penzance to Paignton on 8 October 2020. *Craig Munday*

Below: A 9-car GWR Class 802 set climbs towards Menheniot at Bethany with the 05.58 Plymouth–Penzance on 2 June 2022. *Keith Barrow*

Above: Locomotive Services Ltd 47593 *Galloway Princess* leads 1Z80, the 09.25 *Statesman* excursion from Penzance to Kingswear at Berry Farm Bridge, Bethany, on 26 September 2020. 47805 is at the rear of the train. *Nathan Stockman*

Above: An impressive engineering feature between St Germans and Menheniot is the 795 ft long, 138 ft high Coldrennick Viaduct. DB Cargo 66035 and 66149 cross the structure with a Burngullow–Bow sand train on 25 February 2019. With the closure of Whiteball Tunnel and the diversion of trains via Honiton double-heading was necessary for the 1 in 37 climb between Exeter St Davids and Exeter Central, although the locos remained paired for the entire diagram. These trains were worked from Burngullow to Exeter Riverside yard in two portions, this being the first. Menheniot station is visible on the left, with Bodmin Moor on the horizon. *Nathan Stockman*

Above: Following their introduction in 1999/2000 the Class 67s were briefly a regular sight on mail trains in Cornwall until Royal Mail transferred this traffic to road transport. The class still makes occasional visits to the Duchy, mostly on charter trains. On 29 June 2018 Colas Rail 67027 *Charlotte* – the loco that hauled the last ever Travelling Post Office train through Cornwall on 9 January 2004 – negotiates the reverse curve through Menheniot station with a Network Rail track recording train heading towards Plymouth. The train was operating in place of the usual New Measurement Train (NMT) HST. *Nathan Stockman*

Above: The First Great Western "Local Lines" livery of 150 221 contrasts nicely with the autumnal hues of the landscape at Factory Bridge, Menheniot, as the unit heads east with 2P86, the 10.37 Penzance–Plymouth on 5 November 2016. *Nathan Stockman*

Above: A day of sun and showers sees 158 763 leaning into the curve by Liskeard's down distant signal at Trethawl while working 2C24, the 11.26 Exeter St Davids–Penzance on 1 November 2020. *Craig Munday*

Above: On 14 May 2018 143 621 crosses Bolitho Viaduct working 2E12 Penzance–Exeter St Davids, which had started from Par. The unit had run empty from Exeter to Par to work the service following the failure of the booked 2+4 "Castle" HST set. GWR's Exeter-based Class 143 Pacer DMUs were used on local services in Devon but were infrequent visitors to Cornwall, only making incursions into the Duchy when the booked traction was unavailable. GWR withdrew its final Class 143s in December 2020. *Nathan Stockman*

Above: Having failed at Bodmin Parkway on 31 October 2018, unable to make the climb to Largin, GWR HST set LA60 with power cars 43027 and 43197 returned to Penzance. On 2 November 2018 sleeper locomotive 57603 *Tintagel Castle* was used to haul the set to Plymouth Laira depot for attention. The train is seen at Bolitho with 43027 (with graphics marking the 90th birthday of Queen Elizabeth II) at the front and 43197 at the rear. This was to be the last full-length HST "drag" on the Cornish Main Line. *Nathan Stockman*

Below: On a frosty 23 November 2015 a spectacular sunrise illuminates a GWR Class 153 forming 2C41 Plymouth–Par as it passes signal LD34 at Liskeard. Upon arrival at Par the single-car unit would take up Newquay branch duties from 09.00. *Craig Munday*

Above: The first ever visit of a Class 68 locomotive to Cornwall occurred on 27 May 2016, when 68017 *Hornet* worked a round trip from Exeter to Penzance light engine prior to the class featuring on the *Northern Belle* and Network Rail test trains over the summer. The loco is pictured creeping through Liskeard station – although the quirky LD3 semaphore is "off" the keen eye will see the colour light at the end of the viaduct is "on" as the preceding passenger train is yet to clear the section to St Germans. The line leading off to the left in front of the locomotive is the connection to the Looe branch. *Nathan Stockman*

Above: Colas Rail 70810 crosses over and heads along the up main towards the Looe branch connection at the east end of Liskeard's up platform with 6C35, the 02.50 Aberthaw Cement Works to Moorswater on 10 May 2017. The lack of direct access to the Looe branch from the east meant this train usually continued beyond Liskeard to Lostwithiel, where the loco could run round the train without obstructing the main line. This was only the second time the loaded cement from Aberthaw had run round at Liskeard, the first time being the train's first ever run in November 2016, when it operated with only 15 tanks. The area to the right of the image was once part of the goods yard. *Nathan Stockman*

CHAPTER 3: LISKEARD–PAR

West of Liskeard station the line descends at 1 in 59 to Moorswater Viaduct, one of the most impressive structures on the Cornish Main Line. The 954 ft long, 147 ft high stone viaduct with cast iron parapets, which spans the valley of the East Looe River, was completed in February 1889, replacing Brunel's original timber frame viaduct, which was in use for just 22 years. The piers of the original viaduct still stand immediately to the south of the present structure. The arrival of the Cornwall Railway in the East Looe valley in 1859 was preceded by the opening of the Liskeard & Caradon Railway in 1844. In 1860 the Liskeard & Looe Railway opened with its northern terminus at Moorswater, where it connected with the L&CR.

Above: Having worked to Lostwithiel to run round, 70802 crosses Moorswater Viaduct for the second time with an Aberthaw–Moorswater cement train on 18 April 2018. A few minutes later the train will pass beneath the viaduct to access the former English China Clays facility at Moorswater (visible above the train) where the cement trains from South Wales were unloaded. This drone view clearly shows the surviving masonry piers of Brunel's original 1859 viaduct. The current viaduct was completed in 1881, initially carrying a single broad-gauge track. *Nathan Stockman*

The Cornwall Railway had planned to construct a connection with the Liskeard & Caradon at Moorswater but this was abandoned due to a lack of funds. Passengers travelling into Liskeard alighted at Moorswater until 1896, when a new platform opened at Coombe just south of the viaduct. This provided passengers from Looe with a shorter (but steep) walk into Liskeard. Finally, a connection between the Looe branch and the main line at Liskeard GWR station was completed in 1901, albeit with a reversal at Coombe Junction, which remains to this day. Passenger services between Coombe and Moorswater then ceased, but the line under the viaduct remained open for freight traffic and was last used in 2020 by cement trains from Aberthaw in South Wales.

Beyond Moorswater the main line begins to climb with gradients of up to 1 in 58 past the village of Dobwalls before entering Sperritt Tunnel, the newest tunnel on the Cornish Main Line and one of the shortest. The tunnel was constructed in 2008 as part of the A38 Dobwalls bypass to carry the rerouted A390 across the railway, replacing an underpass with a sharp curve, which was a notorious road accident blackspot. The tunnel was

named in honour of Frank Sperritt, a Cornish signalling engineer and railway enthusiast who was instrumental in the modernisation of signalling infrastructure in the West Country.

The line then passes the site of Doublebois station, which closed to passengers on 5 October 1964 and freight two months later. Today nothing remains to indicate there was once a station here. At Doublebois the line begins its long descent through an area known as the Glynn Valley – Glynn actually means valley in Cornish and the valley is that of the River Fowey, which the Cornish Main Line follows as far as Milltown south of Lostwithiel. The valley is heavily wooded with conifer plantations, and the cycle of tree planting and felling means photographic viewpoints are in constant flux – as one location is consumed by fast-growing vegetation another will be opened up by forestry operations.

The narrow valley provides a natural east-west corridor between Bodmin Moor to the north and the equally undulating landscape to the south. It is therefore a key transport artery between Plymouth and central and western Cornwall, carrying both the railway and the A38. However, this is by no means an easy route

Above: West Coast Railway Company 47804 heads west near Lantoom Quarry with 1Z82, the 08.47 Bristol Temple Meads–Par *Royal Duchy* on 30 August 2020. ***Craig Munday***

Above: With just over a week remaining before the final withdrawal of slam-door Mark 3s (except on sleeper services), FGW blue-liveried 43010 nears the summit below the village of Dobwalls, having been on the climb since Lostwithiel, on 23 December 2019. This power car was retained as part of the Castle fleet, receiving modifications to operate with power doors and GWR green livery before gaining the name *Lydford Castle*. 43010 remained in traffic with GWR until 7 September 2023 and was exported to Nigeria in November 2023. ***Nathan Stockman***

Above: On 13 September 2020 GB Railfreight 66752 *The Hoosier State* and 66761 *Wensleydale Railway Association 25 years* pass Dobwalls top-and-tailing 6G73, the 12.08 Westbury–Lostwithiel "Autoballasters" conveying ballast for renewals on the Fowey branch. GBRf locomotives have never been common in Cornwall but make occasional forays west of the Tamar on engineering trains. *Keith Barrow*

– the road winds its way along the valley floor close to the river while above it the railway clings to the southern slopes of the valley, descending gradients as steep as 1 in 58 and crossing eight viaducts with a combined length of more than two thirds of a mile in the six miles between Doublebois and Bodmin Parkway.

Just beyond Westwood Viaduct (372 ft long, 88 ft high) a rail-served quarry once supplied stone for the reconstruction of the many timber framed viaducts in Cornwall in the late 19th Century. Brunel had warned the Cornwall Railway that while timber viaducts would be cheaper to build they would cost more to maintain. His prediction proved correct and by 1875 the cost of maintaining Cornwall's 42 wooden viaducts exceeded £10 000 a year and it is said that 55 full-time staff were employed in keeping them operational. Replacement work began in 1875 but it would take until the 1930s to complete the rebuilding of all of Cornwall's timber viaducts.

The next two viaducts are among the most impressive in Cornwall and have long been popular with railway photographers. St Pinnock is the tallest viaduct in Cornwall, its 633 ft long deck carrying the railway 151 ft above the valley floor. Designed by Brunel and completed in 1855, the viaduct's seven piers were heightened in 1882, replacing Brunel's original trestles with iron girders.

A little over a third of a mile beyond St Pinnock the curved Largin Viaduct is 567 ft long and 130 ft high. In 1886 the viaduct was rebuilt in a similar manner to St Pinnock, heightening the eight original masonry piers to support iron girders. By the early 1960s British Railways faced the cost of strengthening and renewals on both viaducts and it was therefore decided to single this short stretch of the line in 1964.

As the line continues its descent it crosses five more viaducts: West Largin (315 ft long, 75 ft high), Draw Wood (669 ft long, 42 ft high), Derrycombe (369 ft long, 77 ft high), Clinnick (330 ft long, 74 ft high) and Penadlake (426 ft long, 42 ft high).

Following the closure of the lines to Bodmin General, Wadebridge and Padstow in the 1960s Bodmin Parkway became a railhead for much of North Cornwall. Known as Bodmin Road until November 1983, the station is the junction for the three-mile branch to Bodmin General, which closed to passengers on 30 January 1967 and freight traffic on 20 November 1983, reopening as the Bodmin & Wenford Railway (B&WR) in 1990. Following closure to passengers the line was retained for the transport of china clay from Wenford Bridge on the edge of Bodmin Moor, with trains reversing at Boscarne Junction and Bodmin General to reach the main line. The section between Bodmin General and Boscarne Junction is also now part of the B&WR.

In 2007 the B&WR constructed a carriage shed on the former china clay sidings at the western end of the station, where there is also a connection with the main line. The heritage line uses the northernmost platform face at Bodmin Parkway, providing convenient connections with main line trains.

The current station building on the down platform and the waiting room on the up platform date from 1989, but the fine GWR covered footbridge and the Grade II listed GWR Type 3 signal box on the down platform have survived and remain in use, the latter having been repurposed as a café. The signal box was built in 1887, when the branch to Bodmin General opened and closed in November 1983, when freight traffic ceased on the branch and all signals were removed.

West of Bodmin Parkway the line continues to descend, dropping away from the end of the platform at 1 in 65 as it runs alongside the River Fowey and to the south of the Lanhydrock estate, which is now owned by the National Trust. As it follows the Fowey valley the line passes through the 88 yd Brown Queen Tunnel and briefly heads south-east, passing the ruins of Restormel Castle, one of Cornwall's four main Norman castles (the others being Launceston, Tintagel and Trematon).

As the railway turns to the south goods loops and semaphore signals appear on both sides of the line on the approach to Lostwithiel station. The loops are used by china clay trains, which reverse here to access the branch to Fowey. The 4.75 mile branch closed to passenger traffic in 1965 but remains in use for freight traffic to the china clay export terminal at Carne Point just north of Fowey.

Above: 70802 approaches Sperritt Tunnel with 6C35, the 02.50 Aberthaw–Moorswater cement on 25 January 2017. The tunnel carries the railway under the rerouted A390 road, which previously passed beneath the bridge in this image. *Keith Barrow*

Above: DB Cargo 66136 and 66027 top-and-tail 3S56, the 12.46 Newton Abbot Hackney Yard–St Blazey Railhead Treatment Train (RHTT), across St Pinnock Viaduct on 5 October 2017. The rear loco, 66027, was the first Class 66 to work in Cornwall, arriving in the Duchy on the 14.50 Newport Alexandra Dock Junction–St Blazey "Enterprise" train in tandem with 37683 on 5 January 1999. The RHTT made its debut in Cornwall in 2007, when Colas Rail operated the train using Class 47s. EWS (now DB Cargo) took over in 2008 and remains the operator 15 years later. *Keith Barrow*

Above: Low, strong mid-winter light illuminates 43194 *Okehampton Castle* leading 2C22 Plymouth–Penzance across St Pinnock Viaduct on 18 December 2021. ***Craig Munday***

Above: Cornwall's position on the Atlantic coast means changeable weather conditions can often frustrate the photographer but with a little luck it can also result in dramatic scenes like this. On 1 October 2021, a blustery autumn day with vicious showers, exceptional light and the extremely rare sight of a Class 33 at work on the Cornish Main Line combine at the right moment for a fine shot of WCRC 33207 *Jim Martin* and 37706 crossing Largin East viaduct with 1Z47, the 08.35 Penzance to Plymouth leg of a Steam Dreams charter to London Victoria. ***Craig Munday***

Above: The clearance of an area of forest due to diseased trees opened up a new vantage point for photography across the valley to Largin East Viaduct in late 2022. DB Cargo 66070 is glimpsed crossing the viaduct working empty JIA china clay hoppers back to St Blazey on 24 January 2023. *Craig Munday*

Above: Scrap and fuel traffic ensured the survival of mixed freight trains in Cornwall well into the 2010s although both flows were lost to road transport soon after this 31 May 2013 view. 66172 climbs through the lush Glynn valley approaching the single line section at Largin with five loaded MBA scrap wagons from St Blazey and six discharged TTA fuel tanks from Long Rock depot at Penzance. The train is the Friday-only 6C39 11.50 St Blazey–Alexandra Dock Junction. *Nathan Stockman*

After the loops rejoin the main running lines the railway crosses a level crossing and enters Lostwithiel station. The station is now an unstaffed halt and the buildings have been swept away to be replaced by basic shelters. Until the 1960s passenger trains to Fowey used the eastern side of the down platform and a yard to the south of the down platform remained in use for china clay traffic until the 2000s, later seeing infrequent use by infrastructure trains until it was lifted in 2022. At the level crossing end of the down platform, the 1893-built Lostwithiel signal box has a 63-lever frame. A panel controlling the Largin area was installed in 1991, enabling the closure of Largin signal box. Lostwithiel signal box was due to close in March 2024 and resignalling will sweep away the semaphores at this location.

Heading south out of the station the line crosses the River Fowey. Major works were carried out here in March 2021 to renew the bridge. Eight new deck sections were assembled to the south of the line and lifted into place using a large crane. The Fowey branch diverges immediately south of the bridge and follows the river while the main line begins the climb out of the Fowey valley with gradients of up to 1 in 64. The line crosses the 501 ft long, 75 ft high Milltown Viaduct before reaching the summit inside the 565 yd Treverrin Tunnel. The line then drops sharply towards St Austell Bay, initially descending at 1 in 62 before the gradient eases as the line curves past the village of Tywardreath.

As the line curves round to the south a goods loop diverges from the down line and semaphore signals mark the entry into Par station, junction for the Newquay branch.

The station building is on the down side (Platform 1) while up trains share an island platform with the Newquay line on the west side of the station (Platform 3). Platform 3 can be accessed via both the up and down line. A loop enables trains from the Newquay line to bypass Platform 3 and this is often used by china clay trains. A siding off the loop, accessed from the north end of the station and known as the "Liner Siding" is often used for stabling track machines. South of the station, a second siding runs parallel with the main line and is known as "Chapel Siding" – this is often used to stable DMUs between duties on the Newquay and Looe branches.

At the south end of the island platform is Par signal box. At the time of writing this was the oldest operational signal box in Cornwall, although it was due to close in March 2024 with the resignalling of Lostwithiel–Truro and the transfer of control to Exter signalling centre. Built to the GWR's first standard design, the box was constructed in 1879 with a 26-lever frame and was extended in 1893. The current 57-lever frame dates from 1913. Like the other surviving signal boxes on the Cornish Main Line Par has gradually extended its area through the rationalisation of signalling infrastructure and box closures. A panel controlling the Par–Probus section was installed in 1985 and the box was awarded Grade II listed status in July 2013.

Above: 153 305 and 153 361 cross Clinnick Viaduct with 2C47 14.15 Plymouth–Penzance on 25 March 2017. At this time GWR had 14 Class 153s in its fleet – nine of these units owned by leasing company Angel Trains were due to leave the franchise in May 2017 but delays to the Great Western electrification programme and the planned cascade of Class 166 Turbo units from the Thames Valley meant the "Tin Rockets" remained in the South-West longer than planned. With the Angel Trains units due for a repaint, a contract was awarded to Chrysalis Rail, which treated the vehicles at the former MOD site at Long Marston. The first to emerge, 153305, was returned to GWR in what was officially described as a "neutral livery", which quickly earned the unit the nickname "Casper" for its ghostly appearance.

In late 2023 both units remained in service with different operators – 153 305 has been modified to carry bicycles and is used by ScotRail on the West Highland Line, while 153 361 is with Transport for Wales. *Nathan Stockman*

Above: Having visited Lostwithiel to run round its train, Colas Rail 70806 retraces its steps through the Glynn Valley with 6C35, the 03.10 Aberthaw Cement Works to Moorswater on 3 May 2017, seen here climbing towards Largin. The cement tanks would be unloaded at Moorswater before returning to Aberthaw the following morning. *Nathan Stockman*

Above: Tree growth has made Penadlake Viaduct difficult to photograph from ground level, but here the use of a drone has overcome such obstacles, providing a spectacular view of a Paddington-bound HST crossing the structure on 7 May 2018. *Nathan Stockman*

Above: With Dreasonball Wood crowning the hill in the background CrossCountry 221 124 accelerates away from its Bodmin Parkway stop with 1S47, the 08.28 Penzance–Glasgow Central on 24 May 2012. The photograph was taken from the northern edge of Newbridge Wood after some felling had taken place – a decade on this view has once again disappeared behind vegetation. The A38 is out of sight behind the train – a crash barrier can just be seen to the right of the unit's headlight. *Nathan Stockman*

Above: Late on the evening of Saturday 23 March 2019 GWR 153 361 with no passengers on board calls at a deserted Bodmin Parkway. The train is 2P96, the 22.12 Par to Plymouth, a service that usually started from Newquay, but engineering work saw the branch closed for the weekend. This was the last ever single carriage passenger service in Cornwall. The same unit visited Penzance the following day, albeit coupled with a Class 150, before the class became history in the South-West. *Nathan Stockman*

Above: On a fine evening after a day of heavy rain showers across Cornwall, First Great Western 57605 *Totnes Castle* approaches Respryn Bridge with 2C51, the 17.50 Exeter St Davids–Penzance on 30 June 2014. ***Keith Barrow***

Above: The mist of a chilly midwinter morning in the Fowey valley is beginning to lift as 43002 leads an up HST towards Plymouth at Respryn on 14 January 2018. In 2016 GWR returned two power cars to heritage liveries to mark the 40th anniversary of the introduction of the HSTs on the Western Region. 43002 received the original blue/yellow/grey livery, while 43185 was returned to the InterCity "swallow" scheme carried by the HSTs from the late 1980s until privatisation. ***Craig Munday***

Above: Locomotive Services Ltd 37667 and 37688 *Great Rocks* pass Restormel with the 09.57 Bristol East Yard–Penzance private charter on 4 April 2021. ***Keith Barrow***

Above: No book on Cornwall's railways in the diesel era would be complete without a Class 50 or two, and the "Hoovers" still make occasional forays along the Cornish Main Line on railtours while preserved 50042 is in regular use at the Bodmin & Wenford Railway. Complete with matching blue and grey Mark 2 stock, 50007 *Hercules* and 50049 *Defiance* pass Restormel with 1Z52, Pathfinder Railtours' *Mazey Day Cornishman*, returning from Penzance to Tame Bridge Parkway on 23 June 2018. Both locos now carry GB Railfreight livery. ***Craig Munday***

Above: DB Cargo 66185 *DP World London Gateway* briefly disturbs the tranquillity of a warm autumn afternoon in the Fowey valley at Restormel as it heads east with 6C53, the 15.06 St Blazey–Exeter Riverside china clay on 5 October 2017. **Keith Barrow**

Above: At the eastern end of Lostwithiel loops DB Cargo 66020 runs round its rake of CDA wagons loaded with china clay bound for Fowey Carne Point on 4 November 2020. The CDAs were introduced in 1987 while the Class 66s made their debut on china clay workings to Fowey in 1999. Following the withdrawal of these distinctive wagons in summer 2023 eight CDAs are now preserved at the nearby Bodmin & Wenford Railway. **Craig Munday**

Above: On 14 October 2015 Colas Rail 70804 has just deposited a Railvac in the yard at Lostwithiel, having hauled the machine down from Westbury. Note the recently-installed galvanised "safety cage" on the semaphore signal. The yard was once a busy location for china clay traffic and continued to see use for this purpose until the 2000s. By this time of this photograph the sidings were used only very infrequently for engineering trains and the track was lifted in 2022. *Craig Munday*

Below: On 19 August 2023 DB Cargo 66190 has just arrived in Lostwithiel Down Goods Loop with 6Z73, the 14.32 Exeter Riverside–Par. The first five wagons are ex-Tarmac JGA hoppers, which were resurrected from store to supplement the fleet of JIA hoppers on china clay traffic following the withdrawal of the CDA fleet. Unfortunately, this appears to have been unsuccessful and at the end of 2023 Cornish clay traffic was exclusively handled with the Imerys JIA fleet. *Keith Barrow*

Above: The driver of 66176 working 6G08, the 16.29 Goonbarrow Junction–Carne Point china clay, receives the single-line token for the Fowey branch from the signalman as the train eases out of the down goods loop at Lostwithiel on 11 July 2014. ***Keith Barrow***

Above: A rainbow heralds the imminent arrival of a shower as DB Cargo 66206 rolls into Lostwithiel station with 6G06, the 07.39 Goonbarrow Junction–Fowey Carne Point china clay on 18 August 2017. The loco will run round the train in the loop before setting off back down the Fowey branch, which is guarded by signal LL57 on the left. ***Keith Barrow***

Above: DB Cargo 66165 brings a loaded clay train through Lostwithiel for Fowey on 22 June 2022. The recently lifted china clay sidings and the former Fowey branch platform are visible in the foreground. Since the closure of the St Blazey–Fowey line in 1968 for conversion into a haul road it has been necessary for all trains to and from Carne Point to reverse at Lostwithiel. This operation is usually conducted very efficiently by the traincrew and signaller with clay trains often exiting the loops ahead of schedule. *Nathan Stockman*

Above: With its string of 38 CDAs snaking away behind, 66092 slogs up the bank to Treverrin Tunnel at Milltown with 6G07, the 13.50 Fowey Dock Carne Point to Goonbarrow Junction empties on 9 April 2015. The loco had run round its train at Lostwithiel having come up the Fowey branch, which is behind the trees to the right of the loco. After 35 years of service the final CDAs were withdrawn in August 2023, when they were replaced by JIA bogie hoppers on workings to Fowey. *Nathan Stockman*

Above: Direct Rail Services 37558 (37424) *Avro Vulcan XH 558* crosses Milltown viaduct with Network Rail inspection saloon 975 025 *Caroline* on 25 July 2018. Lostwithiel is visible on the right of the picture. ***Nathan Stockman***

Above: DB Cargo 66150 descends Treverrin Bank towards Par at Treesmill with a rake of empty CDA china clay hoppers forming 6G07, the 13.50 from Fowey Carne Point to St Blazey yard on 23 April 2021. In December 2020 this loco was used for trials with hydrotreated vegetable oil (HVO), a synthetic fuel that significantly reduces carbon dioxide and nitrous oxide emissions when used in diesel engines. ***Nathan Stockman***

Above: Locomotive Services Limited 47805 and 47501 apply the power to lift 1Z90, the Penzance–Oxford *Dreaming Spires Statesman* up Treverrin bank at Tywardreath on 7 May 2022. Note the conical china clay tip in the top right corner of the picture, a prominent feature of the landscape in this area. ***Craig Munday***

Above: On 13 June 2021 66140 and 66120 approach Par top-and-tailing a Network Rail MPV on weedsprayer duty. In 2023 these trains were operated by GB Railfreight. The goods loop behind the train is occasionally used to recess china clay trains. ***Craig Munday***

Above: 43097 *Castle Drogo* leads 2C67, the 08.00 Cardiff Central–Penzance into Par on 29 November 2022 with 43189 *Launceston Castle* at the rear of the train. ***Craig Munday***

Above: 66176 arrives at Par with the 6P07, the 07.26 St Blazey–Parkandillack china clay empties on 27 May 2014 as a Class 221 *Super Voyager* unit pauses with a CrossCountry service from Penzance. The lack of a west-facing chord between the Newquay branch and the main line means the handful of freight trains heading west from St Blazey yard are forced to first run east from Par. Following the departure of the CrossCountry service the Class 66 will ascend Treverrin Bank to reach Lostwithiel, where it will run round the train of CDA hoppers before returning west through Par and St Austell to reach the Parkandillack branch. ***Keith Barrow***

Above: After a long absence Class 158 DMUs became common on the Cornish Main Line once again from May 2018 onwards following the cascade of Class 166 Turbo units from the Thames Valley to the Bristol area. GWR 158 763 calls at Par with 2C47 Plymouth–Penzance on 12 July 2018. By this time 158 763 was the final Class 158 in the colourful First Great Western "Local Lines" livery. This unit was also one of the first Class 158s to be withdrawn after suffering extensive damage in a collision at Salisbury Tunnel Junction on 31 October 2021. *Craig Munday*

Above: A full house at Par on 18 March 2022 with all three platforms occupied. On the left, 150 258 awaits departure with 2N10 to Newquay, 43162 is on the rear of 2P20 Penzance–Plymouth and 802 109 pauses with 1C80 Paddington–Penzance. *Craig Munday*

Above: A view of the interior of Par signal box with its 56-lever frame on 1 March 2023. Par box controls an area from just east of Par station to Probus, a total distance of around 15 miles. The lever frame controls the station area while a panel out of shot to the right controls the St Austell–Probus section. *Craig Munday*

Above: On 26 July 2018 43124 emerges from the shadows at Par with 1A79 06.47 GWR service from Penzance to London Paddington. Behind the power car is Chapel Siding and the line to St Blazey and Newquay curves off to the right behind the signal box. 43124 subsequently joined the ScotRail HST fleet. *Finbarr O'Neill*

CHAPTER 4: PAR–TRURO

Having reached the coast the line begins to head inland again from Par, climbing almost continuously for nearly seven miles to Burngullow Junction. South of Par station the line crosses the short freight-only branch from St Blazey to Par Harbour, which is clearly visible from the train. The line then swings round the west, running parallel with the coastline of Carlyon Bay through the golf links above Shorthorn and Crinnis beaches. The surroundings then become more urban as the line enters St Austell. The remains of the line into St Austell goods yard branching off to the north are still visible, although the yard itself has been redeveloped as the Brunel Business Park. The goods yard opened in 1931, replacing a yard adjacent to the station, and following closure to general goods traffic in 1968 continued to handle household coal traffic until the mid-1980s.

Above: A GWR Castle HST set approaches Par with a service from Penzance on 9 August 2021. The train has just crossed the low viaduct that carries the main line over the freight-only branch from St Blazey to Par Harbour (visible on the left) and the former Cornwall Minerals Railway line to Fowey, which closed in 1968. The route was subsequently rebuilt as a haul road for china clay traffic to Fowey docks. *Finbarr O'Neill*

The line then passes under an unremarkable looking but notable structure. Installed in October 2007, the footbridge between Alexandra Road and Carlyon Road was the first glass fibre-reinforced polymer (FRP) structure on the UK railway network.

After passing beneath Carlyon Road the line enters St Austell, one of Cornwall's busiest stations, which is situated on the northern edge of the town centre. The original station building, constructed in 1859 and rebuilt in 1882, was demolished in 1999 and the new station building was inaugurated on 8 June 2000. The new station footbridge, which is equipped with lifts, was completed in 2015. The original 1882 footbridge was removed in February 2019 and was donated by Network Rail to the Helston Railway. To the north of the platforms, a car park now occupies the site of the former sidings, which were used by Motorail trains from Kensington Olympia until 1984.

To the west of the station, the line passes the derelict 43-lever signal box, closed in 1980, and the site of the junction with the Trenance Valley Line to Lansalson, which served the china clay industry north of St Austell until its closure in 1968. The line then crosses the 618 ft long, 115 ft high St Austell Viaduct, which offers

excellent views over the western end of St Austell as it passes over the Trenance valley. The masonry viaduct replaced the original wooden framed structure in 1899 although the piers of the original viaduct remain in situ.

After crossing the 1898 Gover Viaduct the line passes through Trewoon, a suburb of St Austell, before reaching Burngullow. Once a key location for rail freight operations in Cornwall, the former ECC Blackpool Dryers with its huge buildings and silos now await demolition, the sidings gradually disappearing beneath the buddleia. Production of clay slurry at the Blackpool plant at Burngullow ended in 2003 but Imerys continued to move clay slurry by road from Par Harbour to Burngullow for loading onto trains until January 2008, when the flow of clay slurry to Irvine in Scotland ceased. The disused slurry wagon cleaning shed remains extant more than 15 years after it was last used.

This was not the end of rail freight operations at Burngullow, however, as Methrose Siding at the St Austell end of the complex is still occasionally used for loading aggregate trains and two sidings remain in use for china clay traffic on the freight-only Parkandillack branch – wagons are often brought down from Treviscoe to Burngullow in two portions, before being combined

Above: There was an extremely unusual duty for a GWR Class 57/6 on 27 September 2021 after Colas Rail tamper DR77901 working 6J88 St Austell–Par suffered an altercation with a tree just before the Cypress Avenue bridge at Carlyon Bay. The tamper was disabled and required assistance, which was provided by cancelling the Paddington–Penzance sleeper at Plymouth. 57603 *Tintagel Castle* ran as 1Z99 to Carlyon Bay, where it was coupled to DR77901 before hauling the stricken tamper at 5 mph to Par Chapel Siding. The train is seen dropping down the bank to Par. ***Nathan Stockman***

for the run to Fowey. Freight trains from the branch are also sometimes held here awaiting a path on the main line.

At the western end of the Burngullow site the line passes beneath a road bridge before the branch to Parkandillack curves off sharply to the north. The main line then passes through the site of the second Burngullow station, which opened in 1901 but closed just 30 years later. The signal box remained in use until 1986 when the section of the main line between Burngullow Junction and Probus was singled with control passing to a panel at Par signal box.

From Burngullow Junction the line descends for more than two miles, winding its way into the valley of the River Fal, passing the village of Coombe and crossing the 738 ft long 70 ft high Coombe St Stephen Viaduct, which carries the railway over the Fal. The line then begins its climb to the site of Grampound Road station, crossing the Fal Viaduct, which spans another branch of the same river. The community of Grampound Road grew around the station of the same name but the village of Grampound itself is more than two miles away. The closure of Grampound Road station on 5 October 1964 made the 14.5-mile stretch between St Austell and Truro the longest section of the Cornish Main Line without a station.

The line then descends, initially at 1 in 67 then at 1 in 88 to the site of Probus & Ladock Platform, which opened in 1908 and closed on 2 December 1957. Probus signal box lingered on until August 1965; today no trace of either the station or the signal box remains.

The railway threads its way through the undulating landscape into Truro by means of a series of viaducts and tunnels. Tregarne Viaduct and Tregagle Viaduct date from 1901 and 1902 respectively, replacing the original timber-framed viaducts.

Around half a mile west of Tregagle Viaduct the line passes through the 581 yd Polperro Tunnel and then, 1½ miles to the west, the 320 yd Buckshead Tunnel. The descent into Truro begins inside Buckshead Tunnel, with the line dropping at 1 in 78 to Truro Viaduct, the longest in Cornwall at 1329 ft. Soaring at up to 92 ft above the valley floor, the viaduct provides spectacular views across the city and its cathedral, with the tidal River Truro beyond. A second major viaduct was required to carry the railway across the River Kenwyn; Carvedras Viaduct is 969 ft long and 86 ft high. Between the two viaducts was Cattle Pens Siding, which served the city's cattle market until 1963. There was also a signal box located here.

Truro is Cornwall's busiest station, seeing 1 048 568 entries and exits between April 2021 and March 2022. The original station opened on 4 May 1859 and following the opening of Highertown Tunnel (see Chapter 5) and the completion of the branch to Falmouth in 1863 became an interchange between the broad-gauge Cornwall Railway main line from Plymouth and the standard gauge West Cornwall Railway from Penzance. The WCR was converted to dual gauge in 1866 and broad-gauge passenger trains began running through to Penzance the following year. Both the CR and the WCR were subsequently amalgamated into the GWR and in May 1892 the entire line from Plymouth to Penzance was converted to standard gauge. This enabled the doubling of the line from Truro to Penwithers, as previously the line through Highertown Tunnel had comprised one dual-gauge track for trains to and from Penzance and one broad gauge track for the Falmouth line. Truro station was rebuilt in 1898 and the brick station buildings date from this time.

Above: Unique Citizens' Rail liveried 153325, unusually running singly, works 5P89, the 19.30 Truro–Plymouth along the golf links at Carlyon Bay on 3 June 2015. Citizens' Rail was an EU project to promote regional rail use, which ran from 2012 to 2015. *Craig Munday*

Above: In the final weeks of HST operation on GWR services to and from London, 43172 *Harry Patch – The last survivor of the trenches* sweeps along Carlyon Bay leading 1A85, the 10.00 Penzance–Paddington on 20 April 2019. *Craig Munday*

Above: With loaded JIA bogie wagons conveying china clay from Treviscoe, 66133 is captured running through St Austell at Mount Charles with 6C53, the 14.32 Parkandillack–St Blazey on 30 June 2021. The wagons would remain at St Blazey overnight and then combine with more loaded wagons from Par Harbour before heading to Bescot, then to Cliffe Vale. The red brick commercial building above the wagons stands on the site of St Austell Goods Yard, which was built in the 1930s and remained in use for coal traffic until the mid-1980s, when the remaining traffic was transferred to Drinnick Mill on the Parkandillack branch. *Nathan Stockman*

The station comprises up and down main platforms with a bay platform at the west end of the down platform for branch trains to Falmouth. Unusually the platforms are linked by two footbridges. At the east end of the station, a level crossing provides access to the station car park. Truro is the only station in Cornwall with ticket gates, which were installed following the introduction of half-hourly services on the Falmouth branch. A first class lounge has also been added on the up platform in recent years and the up platform was extended by 9.3 yd (8.5 m) at the Penzance end in October 2021, taking its total length to 240 yd (219 m), enabling it to accommodate 10-car (2x5-car) IET formations.

In addition to the three remaining platforms a fourth platform was used by up trains until 1971, when it became a siding, although this was also removed when the yard was rationalised.

Immediately to the east of the level crossing is Truro signal box, which was due to close in February 2024 as part of the Mid-Cornwall Resignalling Programme, sweeping away the station's fine array of semaphore signals. Originally known as Truro East, the box opened in 1899, replacing two earlier structures. Constructed with a 45-lever frame, it was expanded to 51 levers in 1971 when Truro West box closed.

As late as the 1980s Truro remained a relatively busy location for freight traffic, but with the phasing out of vacuum braked stock, the withdrawal of loss-making freight flows and the demise of Speedlink its role quickly diminished. The link from the yard to the main line at the eastern end of the station was removed in 1988 and today Truro yard has been reduced to two long sidings and one short siding at the west end, which can only be accessed from the western end of the station, and most of the site is occupied by the station car park. The sidings are still used occasionally for stabling engineering and charter trains.

The area to the north of the main line at the western end of the station was once occupied by Truro shed, which was built in 1900 and closed to steam traction in March 1962. Facilities for diesel traction were added in 1959, but the depot closed completely in October 1965. Following the demolition of the shed a rail-connected fertiliser depot was established on the site in 1973 by Shellstar (later UKF Fertilisers) and this continued to receive fertiliser by rail from Ince & Elton in Cheshire until it closed in the 1990s. The rails remain in situ but the connection to Truro yard is out of use.

Above: Following a problem with the DBSO, Colas Rail 37175 finds itself leading 3Q51, the 20.20 Penzance–Exeter Riverside New Yard track inspection train at St Austell on 30 September 2021, an evening later than scheduled. During its BR career this loco had a brief association with Cornwall in 1986/87, when it was based at St Blazey depot for china clay duties. *Craig Munday*

Above: An earlier view of St Austell station showing the 1882 footbridge. 43197 arrives at the head of 1A83 Penzance–Paddington on 6 September 2015. This was one of the GWR power cars that did not go on to a second career following the end of HST operation out of Paddington and after yielding spare parts for the Castle fleet at Plymouth Laira depot 43197 was dispatched to Sims Metals at Newport Docks for scrap on 31 May 2022. *Craig Munday*

Above: On 15 June 2015 DB Schenker 66118 approaches St Austell with 6C10, the 12.53 Burngullow–Exeter Riverside, conveying sand ultimately destined for Bow in East London. This was the first time the train had run since 2013. The loaded train of four-wheel MEA wagons ran to Exeter Riverside yard as two portions, this being the first. The use of MEAs on this occasion was notable as bogie wagons were usually employed on this working. ***Keith Barrow***

Above: Making a rare appearance for a Class 59 in Cornwall, GB Railfreight 59003 *Yeoman Highlander* approaches St Austell with 0Z62, the 11.29 Penzance–Plymouth route learning trip on 15 July 2021. ***Nathan Stockman***

Above: The low winter sun and dark clouds provide dramatic lighting conditions as DB Cargo 66018 crosses Trenance Viaduct with 6P24, the 15.25 Parkandillack–Fowey Carne Point china clay on 8 January 2021. This attractive view across the Gover valley from Trewiddle south of St Austell has since been marred by a new housing development on the fields in the foreground. The tower block on the right is the 11-storey 120 ft Park House, which dates from the 1960s. *Craig Munday*

Above: Adorned with "Visit Plymouth" promotional graphics 43163 leads 1A83 Penzance–Paddington across Gover Viaduct on 15 April 2015. This power car is now part of the ScotRail fleet. *Craig Munday*

Above: 66104 accelerates away from Burngullow Junction with 6C53, the 11.51 Parkandillack–Exeter Riverside on 22 April 2021. The train started from Treviscoe and conveys china clay in JIA bogie hoppers ultimately bound for the Cliffe Vale terminal near Stoke-on-Trent. *Keith Barrow*

Below: Bringing a welcome splash of colour to the sand train, DB Cargo 66162 *Maritime Intermodal Five* awaits departure from Burngullow with 6C12, the 10.28 to Exeter Riverside on 29 August 2019. The JNA wagons have been loaded at Methrose Siding at the eastern end of Burngullow yard and are ultimately destined for Bow in east London. *Craig Munday*

Above: On 22 June 2018 66031 prepares to uncouple from its loaded rake of CDA china clay wagons before returning up the Parkandillack branch to Treviscoe to load the second portion. The train is standing alongside the disused Blackpool Dryers (named after the clay pit to the north and closed in November 2007) with the huge buildings and silos now awaiting demolition. The shed to the right of the locomotive was erected in 1989 for cleaning the interiors of the ICA "Silver Bullet" wagons introduced that year to convey clay slurry to Irvine in Scotland for use in paper production. The shed became redundant when clay slurry traffic from Cornwall to Scotland ceased in January 2008. *Nathan Stockman*

Above: Hauling spare FGW Mark 3 coaches 17175 and 10232 from Penzance depot to Plymouth, 57604 *Pendennis Castle* passes the site of Burngullow station (closed 14 September 1931) on 19 April 2014. This was the fourth run of this working to provide Penzance drivers with main line Class 57 experience in preparation for a summer Saturday diagram to/from Exeter. The line curving sharply to the right is the freight-only branch to Treviscoe and Parkandillack. *Nathan Stockman*

Above: For many years the only regular freight traffic west of Burngullow Junction was the weekly train of fuel oil from St Blazey to Long Rock depot at Penzance. This traffic, which was conveyed in four-wheel TTA tanks, switched to road transport in November 2013. China clay workings dominate the landscape at Crugwallins just west of Burngullow Junction as 66149 heads west with 6C21, the Wednesday-only 12.00 St Blazey–Long Rock on 25 July 2012. *Nathan Stockman*

Above: The transfer of 153 325 and 153 333 from London Midland to First Great Western in 2011 brought some welcome variety and colour to the DMU fleet in Cornwall, with both units retaining the livery of their former franchise for some time after their move to the West Country. 153 325 and 150 261 pass Lower Dowgas with 2C48, the 15.57 Plymouth–Penzance on 8 September 2014. 150 261 had recently been repainted in a more austere version of First Great Western livery, which replaced the attractive "Local Lines" scheme on the operator's DMUs. *Nathan Stockman*

Above: The influence of the gulf stream on Cornwall's climate ensures significant snowfall is a rarity, but on the morning of 17 January 2023 much of the Duchy awoke to a winter wonderland, with clear skies providing excellent photographic conditions for a few hours before the snow melted. 43189 *Launceston Castle* leads 2P13 Penzance–Plymouth through the reverse curve at Dowgas. *Craig Munday*

Above: Autumnal tints in the trees indicate the summer Saturday GWR loco-hauled season is drawing to a close as 57605 *Totnes Castle* crosses the 738 ft long Coombe St Stephens Viaduct with a four-coach 5P70 Penzance–Par empty stock move on 27 August 2016. From Par the train would form a service to Exeter St Davids, returning to Penzance in the evening. By this time, a year after the introduction of the new GWR livery, only three *Night Riviera Sleeper* vehicles (one Restaurant First Modular and two Tourist Standard Open Disabled coaches) remained in FGW blue livery. *Craig Munday*

Above: For much of the period covered by this book poor availability of the small GWR Class 57/6 fleet forced the operator to hire Class 57s from elsewhere, with Direct Rail Services Class 57/3s often being drafted in, sometimes for long periods. DRS 57303 *Pride of Carlisle* passes Trenowth with 5Z40, the 09.20 Penzance T&RSMD–London Paddington empty sleeper stock on 12 September 2015. *Keith Barrow*

Below: 43047 leads the Locomotive Services Limited Midland Pullman set and 43046 through the heatwave-parched landscape at Resparveth between St Austell and Truro with 1Z12, the 06.00 Eastleigh–Penzance *Cornish Coastal Pullman* on 13 August 2022. This was the only train of the day on this section of the Cornish Main Line due to a 24-hour strike by ASLEF members. Above the train is the village of Grampound Road and beyond it the hills of Clay Country. *Keith Barrow*

Above: On 16 May 2019 43009 heads west near Probus leading 1C84 Paddington–Penzance, the final daylight down HST from London to Cornwall. Following the end of HST operation to and from Paddington 43009 was retained by GWR as part of the Castle fleet, receiving the name *Nunney Castle*. Earlier in its long career this power car was also one of the first to be re-engined with an MTU power unit (with 43004). In November 2023 43009 was one of six ex-Castle power cars to be exported to Nigeria. ***Craig Munday***

Above: Tree growth and lack of public access mean there are few photographic locations between Probus and Truro. A clear high summer evening provided the photographer with an opportunity for this view of an unidentified CrossCountry Class 221 *Super Voyager* unit passing through the cutting near Polperro Tunnel with a Penzance-bound service on 16 June 2015. ***Craig Munday***

Above: 150 123 and 150 266 emerge from Buckshead Tunnel with 2C48, the 15.57 Plymouth–Penzance all stations service on 19 June 2015. At the time this busy early evening commuter service was usually a 3- or 4-car DMU formation but was subsequently taken over by GWR Castle HST sets. *Craig Munday*

Above: DB Cargo 66113 and 66097 (closest to the camera) cross Truro Viaduct with 3J13, the Par–St Blazey via Penzance Railhead Treatment Train on 8 October 2023. The unusual building in the foreground is Truro Crown Court. *Keith Barrow*

Above: On 6 October 2023 43098 *Walton Castle* and 43156 *Maen Castle* (closest to camera) working with Mark 3 set GW05 cross Carvedras Viaduct with 2U32, the 16.50 Penzance–Cardiff Central. The skyline is dominated by Truro Cathedral, which was completed in 1910 and is one of only three cathedrals in the United Kingdom with three spires, the others being Lichfield Cathedral and St Mary's Cathedral in Edinburgh. *Finbarr O'Neill*

Below: A 9-car Class 802/1 unit crosses Carvedras Viaduct as it accelerates away from Truro station with a morning Penzance–Paddington service on 17 June 2022. *Finbarr O'Neill*

Above: At 01.20 on 16 November 2014 56113 prepares to back its train of ten MHA Coalfish wagons into the Highertown Tunnel engineers possession at Truro having just run round the train, which it had hauled from Exeter Riverside Yard. This was the first visit of a Colas Class 56 beyond Par/St Blazey and the first use of the class on an engineering train in the Duchy. The same evening 56103/56303 were at Lostwithiel with the "Railvac", the first time three Class 56s had been in Cornwall simultaneously. *Nathan Stockman*

Above: Celebrity power car 43185 *Great Western* leads 1A82, the 09.30 Penzance–Paddington through the semaphores into Truro station on 7 July 2018. The semaphores survived until the resignalling of Truro station in February 2024, which resulted in the closure of the signal box. The industrial buildings behind the train stand on the site of the former Truro locomotive shed and the large shed in the centre of the image was previously the UKF Fertilisers depot, which was rail served until the 1990s. The line on the left leads into the bay platform (Platform 1), which is used by branch trains to Falmouth Docks. *Keith Barrow*

Above: The 51-lever frame in Truro signal box. The box dates from 1899 and was due to close in February 2024 as part of the Mid-Cornwall Resignalling Programme. *Craig Munday*

Below: Having failed earlier in the morning while working the Falmouth branch, London Midland-liveried 153 325 awaits attention in the yard at Truro on 15 April 2014. To the right of the HST arriving from Penzance is signal T26, installed in 2009 as part of capacity enhancement works on the Falmouth branch to enable passenger trains to run from the up main platform to the down main line. Truro West signal box, which closed on 7 November 1971, was situated in front of where the blue building in the centre of the image now stands. *Keith Barrow*

Below: Class 60s were often used on china clay workings in the 1990s and early 2000s, primarily on the Burngullow–Irvine clay slurry trains, which they took over from pairs of Class 37s in July 1995. Following the arrival of EWS' new Class 66s at St Blazey depot in 1999 EMD power became the norm for china clay trains and the Class 60s gradually disappeared from Cornwall. The "Tugs" were never common west of Burngullow, although they made occasional appearances on the St Blazey–Long Rock (Penzance) fuel oil tanks.

Following the purchase of ten locos by Colas Rail in 2014 the class made several forays into Cornwall on engineering duties, although this revival was short lived with the sale of the locos to GB Railfreight in 2018. On 22 January 2016 60047 waits to reverse out of Truro yard with a Railvac returning to Westbury following overnight engineering work. Coupled up and ready to go, the formation stands in the yard while the crew arrange an earlier departure. These sidings now only see occasional use for to stabling engineering and charter trains. *Nathan Stockman*

Right: Most Class 37 activity on Network Rail metals in Cornwall takes place in the hours of darkness, when the veteran English Electric machines work track recording trains on the main line and the branches. Photographing these operations therefore generally requires a visit to a station in the early hours of the morning. Direct Rail Services 37608 pauses at Truro on 22 May 2015 prior to leading an ultrasonic test train to Falmouth Docks. 37607 at the other end of the train had led the formation from St Erth after visiting St Ives. Following its trip down the Falmouth branch the train visited the freight-only Parkandillack branch before leaving Cornwall for Bristol. These duties were subsequently taken over by Colas Rail (p54) and remain in the hands of Class 37s, albeit with push-pull operation using a Network Rail DBSO. Following its sale by DRS in 2016, 1961-built 37608 remains in main line use with the Rail Operations Group and carries Europhoenix livery. *Nathan Stockman*

CHAPTER 5: TRURO–PENZANCE

From Truro station trains heading west immediately face a 1 in 60 climb as the line curves sharply to the south-west and enters the 70 yd Highertown Tunnel. At this point it is worth mentioning the history of the rather curious railway geography in the Truro area. The West Cornwall Railway opened its single-track standard gauge line from the western outskirts of Truro to Penzance in 1852. Penwithers was the temporary and rather inconveniently located terminus of the West Cornwall Railway between 1852 and 1855, when the line to Newham on Truro's riverfront was completed.

Above: 43175 *GWR 175th Anniversary* leads 1A81, the 08.39 Penzance–Paddington GWR service through Penwithers Junction and into Highertown Tunnel on the approach to Truro on 4 June 2016. The branch to Falmouth is visible above the rear of train. Following the introduction of GWR's IETs 43175 joined the ScotRail HST fleet. ***Keith Barrow***

In 1846 parliamentary assent was granted for the Cornwall Railway from Plymouth to Falmouth, which would be part-funded by the GWR and built to Brunel's broad gauge. Construction started near Truro in August 1847 but the scheme quickly became mired in a financial crisis. The contractor for the Truro–Falmouth section collapsed and it was decided to halt work on the line to Falmouth and concentrate resources on building the Plymouth–Truro line, which was completed in May 1859. The opening of Highertown Tunnel connected the WCR with the CR's station (the site of today's Truro station) and passenger services to Newham ceased in 1863, although the branch remained in use for freight traffic until 1971 and is now a footpath.

The railway would not reach Falmouth until 1863, by which time the WCR had been converted to dual gauge and had effectively become the main line. This explains why the Falmouth branch runs on a straight alignment from Highertown Tunnel through Penwithers Junction to the south-west, but the Penzance line curves off sharply to the west, joining the alignment of the original WCR route.

From Penwithers Junction the line begins the three mile 1 in 80 climb to Penstraze, crossing the 372 ft Penwithers Viaduct, which was completed in 1887. After crossing Chacewater and Blackwater Viaducts the line reaches the site of Chacewater station, formerly the junction of the meandering branch to St Agnes, Perranporth and Newquay, which closed on 7 February 1963. Chacewater station lingered on until 5 October 1964 but the signal box remained in use until 1977 and the cement distribution depot in the station yard continued to receive trains from the Blue Circle works at Plymstock until February 1987, the connection with the main line finally being removed in September 1992. Nearly 60 years after the station closed to passengers the down platform remains surprisingly intact.

West of Chacewater station a third track used by trains to and from Newquay ran parallel with the main line as far as Blackwater Junction – the embankments that once carried the branch north towards St Agnes are still clearly visible from the train, but have been severed by the A30 dual carriageway, which runs immediately parallel to the main line for around half a mile. As the road and railway part company the line begins to descend, passing the remains of Hallenbeagle copper mine, a local landmark that for decades has been a popular location for railway photographers.

The line then passes the site of Scorrier station, which closed on 5 October 1964, before crossing a narrow overbridge. Built in around 1852, this structure carried the WCR over the Poldice

Above: In Spring 2016 the first production HST power car, 43002, was restored to its original blue/grey/yellow livery and named *Sir Kenneth Grange* in honour of the designer of the famous cab shape to mark the 40th anniversary of the introduction of the production HSTs. On a beautiful crisp autumnal morning 43002 leads GWR-liveried Mark 3 set LA16 and Intercity-liveried 43185 through the reverse curve at Penstraze forming 1A81, the 08.44 Penzance–London Paddington on 14 October 2016. *Keith Barrow*

Tramroad, the first mineral railway in Cornwall. Opened in around 1815, the horse-drawn plateway linked mines in the Gwennap district south-east of Scorrier with the harbour at Portreath on the north coast. By the time the WCR opened, the four mile tramroad was technically obsolete and traffic was dwindling, resulting in its closure in the 1860s. Today much of the route is a cycleway and a plaque on the wall of the bridge at Scorrier marks its historical significance.

As the line curves round to the south on the approach to Redruth it passes an industrial estate constructed on the site of Drump Lane sidings. The yard opened in 1911 and remained in use for local goods traffic until 1979 – thereafter the loop remained in use as a run-round facility for empty cement trains from Chacewater. The sidings and signal box closed in January 1986.

After passing through the 47 yd Redruth Tunnel, the line enters Redruth station. Opened in 1852, the station had two platforms from the outset and was initially a crossing loop on the WCR's single-track line from Penzance to Truro. The original station building on the up platform was replaced by a brick building in 1930, and this remains in use with facilities including a waiting room and ticket office, toilets and a buffet. On the down platform an older wooden shelter with a waiting room provides protection from the elements. The two platforms are linked by an attractive 1888 GWR footbridge.

The line continues to curve round to the west on a tall embankment immediately south of the town centre before crossing the 1888 Redruth Viaduct. This was built to replace an earlier single-track timber viaduct and initially carried a single dual gauge track until conversion to standard gauge in 1892, which allowed the doubling of the line in 1894. Like the viaducts at St Austell and Truro, Redruth Viaduct provides the passenger with fine views across the town and towards the north coast.

To the west of the viaduct was Redruth Junction where the route meets the alignment of the original Hayle Railway (HR). The HR was a standard-gauge mineral railway built to carry ore from the mines in the Redruth area to the harbour and foundry at Hayle. The section from Portreath Junction to Redruth's original station, a terminus on the western edge of the town just north of the current main line, opened to goods traffic in June 1838. From May 1843 the HR began carrying passengers to Redruth by coupling coaches to the rear of goods trains, but this arrangement was short-lived and the railway closed in 1852 for reconstruction as part of the WCR route from Penzance to Truro. The original HR terminus remained in use as a goods yard until 1968.

To the south of Redruth Junction the Tresavean Tramway connected mines south of the town with the HR via a 1 in 15 rope incline, which closed in 1935. A mile to the west the main line passes Portreath Junction, where the HR line to Portreath (closed 1938) branched off to the north.

The line continues towards Penzance along the northern fringe of the industrial area west of Redruth in the shadow of Carn Brea, a hill rising to 738 ft asl and crowned with the 90 ft monument to Francis Basset, 1st Baron de Dunstanville and Basset, immediately to the south. After passing the site of Carn Brea station, closed on 2 January 1961, the line begins an almost continuous descent to the Hayle estuary around eight miles away.

Evidence of the area's rich mining history is abundant between Redruth and Camborne, with the remains of numerous engine houses visible from the train. A notable local landmark to the north of the line just west of the Carn Brea station site is the pit head of South Crofty, Cornwall's last operational tin mine, which ceased production in 1998. Current owner Cornish Metals is working to reopen the mine, although it is unclear when production will resume.

Roskear Junction signal box opened in 1895 and originally had a 29-lever frame, which was replaced with a panel in 1970, when Camborne signal box closed and Roskear Junction took over control of the area. Roskear Junction also controlled access to the freight-only Roskear branch, the remnants of which were latterly a private siding for the factory of Holman Brothers, a manufacturer of mining machinery and compressors. The branch closed in January 1981.

The closure of Drump Lane signal box at Redruth in 1986 resulted in a 14-mile block section on this stretch of the Cornish Main Line. This was remedied in 2018, when new signal sections with axle counters were installed to enable half-hourly operation, providing a signal at least every six miles. The additional signals in the Redruth and Camborne area are controlled from Roskear, where a new panel was installed as part of the project. Level crossings between Truro and St Erth were also upgraded with Dolcoath becoming the first level crossing in Cornwall to be equipped with obstacle detection.

Camborne station gained fame for "This Train Don't Stop Camborne Wednesdays", a routine by Cornish comedian Jethro, who was commemorated with the unveiling of a memorial plaque at the station in February 2023. Camborne has two platforms, which are connected by a footbridge adjacent to Trevu Road level crossing at the east end of station. The station building, which remains in railway use, dates from around 1900 and is located on the up platform. Unfortunately for passengers the awnings were removed many years ago and the only protection from the elements is provided by basic shelters on both platforms.

The former goods yard on the south side of the station is now a car park and the goods shed has been repurposed as a kitchen retailer's showroom.

Looking west from the platforms at Camborne there is a noticeably steep descent as the line drops away to the west over a distance of around a mile, initially at 1 in 67 then briefly 1 in 55 – one of the most severe gradients on the Cornish Main Line – followed by 1 in 61.

To cross the valley at Penponds the HR originally built an incline but with the construction of the WCR this was replaced by a wooden viaduct in 1852. This soon proved unsatisfactory due to the increasing weight of rolling stock and the viaduct was strengthened and modified several times, which included extending the embankment and shortening the structure. A more permanent solution in the form of a masonry and brick viaduct was completed in 1889. Some of the bridge abutments of the original HR incline survive in Mill Road in Penponds village more than 170 years after closure.

Gwinear Road was the junction for the branch to Helston, which closed to passengers on 3 September 1962 and to goods on 5 October 1964, when the station also closed. This is a particularly productive area for the cultivation of vegetables such as broccoli and potatoes and a small yard between the main line and the Helston line once handled the significant volumes of perishables brought up the branch. All trace of the yard and the branch at this location have been eradicated from the landscape, although the station's island platform on the down side of the main line survives and despite the encroaching vegetation is clearly visible from passing trains.

One of the most impressive viaducts on the western section of the Cornish Main Line soars up to 100 ft over the village of Angarrack, the 798 ft long structure crossing the narrow valley of the Angarrack River on 11 arches. Prior to the construction of the WCR the HR used an incline to move its wagons in and out of the valley on an alignment to the north of the village. From 1843 until the completion of the WCR nine years later a stationary steam engine was used to power the incline. For this reason, the lane from the neighbouring village of Connor Downs, which crosses the alignment of the HR at the top of the incline, is still known as Steamers Hill.

The main line then crosses the 384 ft long, 56 ft high Guildford Viaduct. The six-arch viaduct was completed in 1886 and a century later provided a convenient means of threading the A30 Hayle Bypass under the railway without the expense of building a new bridge.

Hayle station is effectively an unstaffed halt and passenger facilities have been pared back to the absolute minimum, with a basic shelter on each of the two platforms and little else. A footpath curving off to the north behind the up platform follows the route of the Hayle Wharves branch, which diverged from the main line between the western end of the up platform and Hayle Viaduct. The branch, which had a maximum gradient of 1 in 30, served a power station, explosives factory and an oil depot, as well as various sidings in the harbour area. The branch survived well into the diesel era and although a Class 52 and a Class 37 visited on test runs freight traffic was usually handled by a Class 22 diesel-hydraulic or later a Class 25. The power station closed in 1977 but oil and chemical traffic lingered on until January 1981. The branch was taken out of use on 7 July 1982, when the distinctive 1912 signal box on the up platform at Hayle station also closed.

Continuing our journey towards Penzance, the line curves around the south west across Hayle viaduct. The current structure, which dates from 1899, has 36 masonry piers with a deck of longitudinal riveted plate girders supporting transverse timber decking and ballasted track. With a height of only 34 ft it is far from the tallest viaduct in Cornwall but it offers excellent views of the harbour, the Hayle Estuary and the north coast. On the south side of the viaduct is Foundry Square, where the original terminus of the HR was located. Following the opening of the WCR the stretch of the HR along Penpol Terrace to Foundry Square, which passed beneath the viaduct, was retained for goods traffic and wagons were hauled by horses until closure in the 1960s.

After passing through a short cutting, the line swings round to the south and runs alongside the Hayle Estuary, with Lelant and Lelant Saltings stations on the St Ives branch visible on the opposite bank, before turning west once more, passing beneath the A30 Hayle Bypass. The line begins to climb again with a gradient of 1 in 70 on the approach to St Erth station.

Known as St Ives Road until the opening of the 4¼ mile branch to St Ives on 1 June 1877, St Erth station is located around three quarters of a mile from the village of the same name. St Erth is a busy railhead for a large area of West Cornwall and the station has been adapted to modern requirements in recent years with the £10 million St Erth Mutimodal Hub project (see Chapter 1). This has seen the construction of a new car park to the south of

Above: With work in progress on a new lineside fence, 6C99, the 10.00 Penzance–Westbury continuous welded rail train, snakes through Penstraze behind Colas Rail 70817 on 9 November 2022. The train was running 87 minutes late due to a points failure at Penzance. ***Keith Barrow***

Above: 57604 *Pendennis Castle* approaches the site of Chacewater station with 3A50, the 10.44 Penzance T&RSMD–Exeter St Davids empty GWR sleeper stock on 25 February 2022. Immediately behind the loco a third track ran parallel with the main line from Chacewater station to Blackwater Junction, where the branch to Perranporth and Newquay diverged. This was removed following the closure of the Newquay line in 1963. ***Keith Barrow***

the station, which has enabled it to take over the park and ride role for the St Ives branch from Lelant Saltings, which is situated in a residential area further from the A30.

Passenger numbers on the St Ives branch have surged in recent years and during the busy summer months the half-hourly shuttle service is operated by a pair of Class 150 DMUs, providing a 4-car formation. Branch services operate from a bay platform (Platform 3) on the north side of the station, which is at a lower level than the two main line platforms due to the falling gradient on the main line towards Hayle. The bay platform was extended by 6 metres (20 ft) in 2022 to enable the operation of 5-car trains on the St Ives branch.

The Grade II listed granite station building is located on the north side of the main line and houses a ticket office (upgraded in 2017), a waiting area and café.

Following the resignalling in mid-Cornwall St Erth will be one of the last bastions of manual signalling in the Duchy and the lower quadrant semaphores will remain in operation for a few more years yet. Between the main line and the St Ives branch is St Erth signal box, which was built in 1899, replacing a temporary structure erected in 1894. The box was originally fitted with a 55-lever frame but was expanded to the current 69 levers in 1929.

St Erth was once notable for milk traffic originating from the Primrose Dairy (later United Dairies and Unigate), which opened in 1936 adjacent to the up goods yard. Milk trains continued to run daily to London until the traffic ceased on 31 March 1980.

The 1 in 67 climb out of St Erth is the last notable gradient before the line begins its final descent towards Mounts Bay and Penzance. As the line passes the RSPB's Marazion Marshes nature reserve St Michael's Mount and the south coast come into view. Marazion station was the most westerly victim of the cull that saw the closure of six stations on the Cornish Main Line on 5 October 1964. While the platforms are long gone, the building on the down side survives.

With the station's proximity to the beach, camping coaches became a fixture at Marazion from 1937 onwards and from 1963 the area between the station building and the beach was occupied by six former Pullman cars. These were used as holiday accommodation, but suffered from vandalism and the coastal weather, with a hurricane force storm in 1987 proving to be the final straw. However, two of the coaches (*Mimosa* and *Alicante*) were rescued in 1999 and are now used as bedrooms at a bed and breakfast at Petworth station on the former Pulborough–Midhurst line in West Sussex.

The six-siding yard to the north of the main line at Marazion was once an important hub for the movement of agricultural produce from West Cornwall – in 1937 more than 35 000 tonnes

of broccoli were loaded onto trains in the yard here. However, intense competition from road transport after World War II resulted in a rapid decline in perishables traffic and the yard closed on 6 December 1965.

The line west of Marazion was singled by BR in 1974. Around half a mile from the site of Marazion station is Long Rock, which for more than a century has been the centre of locomotive and rolling stock maintenance at the western extremity of the Cornish Main Line. With the growth of traffic the cramped two-road engine shed at Penzance station had become inadequate by the early 20th Century and in 1914 the GWR opened a new four-road shed at Long Rock. Diesel traction arrived in 1958 and the depot closed to steam in September 1962, but the steam shed remained in use until June 1976. A new smaller depot with a 750 ft long maintenance shed designed to accommodate HST sets and officially known as Penzance T&RSMD (depot code PZ) was built on the site and opened in October 1977. With the transfer of the sleeper fleet from Old Oak Common depot and the introduction of half-hourly services more maintenance capacity was required at Long Rock and the depot was extensively rebuilt in 2017–19 (see Chapter 1).

Just to the west of Long Rock is Ponsandane, where for many decades a yard and loading dock was located. After years of disuse and dereliction the site is being revived with the construction of three new sidings to stable 9- and 10-car IET trains, further increasing capacity at Long Rock and reducing the need for empty stock movements between Penzance and Plymouth Laira depot.

When the WCR opened in 1852 the line accessed Penzance station by means of the 1047 ft long 12 ft high Penzance Viaduct. This was extremely vulnerable to Atlantic storms and just a few months after opening a 180 ft section was swept away in December 1852. A further storm in 1868 destroyed more than half of the viaduct and repeated attempts were made to strengthen and improve the structure. However, with its continuing vulnerability to the sea and the introduction of larger locomotives the GWR eventually admitted defeat and constructed an embankment, which was opened

Below: Cornwall's main trunk road, the A30, and the Cornish Main Line run parallel for around half a mile between Blackwater and Scorrier, the dual carriageway slicing through the earthworks of the triangular junction that once linked the Chacewater–Newquay branch with the main line. 43092 *Cromwell's Castle* nears the summit of the climb from the site of Chacewater station with 2C30, the 15.47 Plymouth–Penzance GWR service on 16 March 2022. ***Keith Barrow***

Above: On 24 June 2023 GB Railfreight 69006 *Pathfinder Railtours* and 69006 *Eastleigh* approach Apex Bridge at Scorrier with the return 1Z70 Penzance–Tame Bridge Parkway *Mazey Day Cornishman*. **Craig Munday**

to traffic in July 1921. This is protected from the sea by a parapet rising 3 ft above rail height and beyond sea defences constructed using granite blocks. Works were recently carried out at Long Rock Beach to strengthen the defences.

As the line enters Penzance station it passes the signal box, which is situated to the north of the railway. The current signal box opened in April 1938 and was fitted with a 75-lever frame, part of which remains in use despite the introduction of colour light signalling and hydraulic point motors in December 1981.

Located on the sea front, Penzance station is 326 miles and 50 chains from London Paddington via Box and Plymouth Millbay. The southernmost station on Britain's main line network has expanded significantly since the WCR opened its terminus on 11 March 1852. The original station was a modest facility, comprising just a single platform with a small trainshed, a two-road engine shed, a goods shed, and a siding extending along Albert Quay. This situation persisted even after the conversion of the line to dual gauge, which enabled broad-gauge trains to reach Penzance from 1866. However, the takeover of the WCR by the GWR in 1876 prompted a significant expansion of the station, which was extended westward towards the town centre with two platforms with a centre track for stabling stock. Protection from the elements was provided by a 250 ft long overall roof and the dressed granite station building provided much improved facilities for passengers and staff.

With the conversion of the GWR from broad- to standard-gauge the dual gauge in west Cornwall was abolished, enabling the widening and lengthening of the platforms as well as the construction of a fourth track.

With both freight and passenger traffic continuing to grow, in the late 1930s the GWR embarked on a huge land reclamation project with a new sea wall allowing the expansion of the station site. The goods shed was demolished and platforms were built on the southern side of the site for perishables traffic. The number of passenger platforms was increased from two to four and these were lengthened significantly. The fourth platform was outside the overall roof and was often used by mail trains as it had direct road access.

A travel centre opened inside the train shed as part of the refurbishment of the station in 1980, replacing the booking office. There is also a First Class lounge, which can be used by passengers who have booked berths for the *Night Riviera Sleeper*.

The track layout was rationalised in 1987, when the loading docks were removed; this area is now a car park although a few sidings have been retained on this side of the station and are often used for stabling Network Rail infrastructure measuring trains.

The fastest journey time to Paddington in the Summer 2023 timetable was 4h52, although only a single train in each direction, the 05.03 Penzance–Paddington and the 10.04 Paddington–Penzance, offered journey times of less than five hours.

Just beyond the buffer stops on Platform 4 south of the station building a large sign carved from a block of Cornish granite is engraved with the bilingual greeting "Penzance Welcomes You" and below it in Cornish "PENSANS A 'GAS DYNERGH" was erected in the early 1990s, a fitting finale for a trip along the beautiful Cornish Main Line.

Above: Once part of part of Hallenbeagle copper mine, Reed's Shaft Engine House is a landmark on the Cornish Main Line that has been popular with railway photographers for many decades, the adjacent level crossing providing an excellent vantage point for down trains. GWR 57605 *Totnes Castle* passes the imposing 1864-built structure with 5C99, the 11.00 Reading Traincare Depot–Penzance T&RSMD empty sleeper stock on 14 March 2022. This was the location of Wheal Busy siding, which acted as a goods yard for Scorrier station until its closure in 1963. In March 2018 remediation work was carried out during an engineering blockade at this location to safeguard the railway from historic mine workings beneath the trackbed. ***Keith Barrow***

Above: In the final rays of evening sunshine on 5 August 2017 43304 leads 1V58, the 09.00 Glasgow Central–Penzance CrossCountry service approaching the now-closed Wheal Prussia foot crossing at Treleigh. By this time this Summer Saturday turn was the only booked CrossCountry HST working in west Cornwall. Following the withdrawal of the CrossCountry HST fleet 43304 was exported to Nigeria in November 2023. ***Keith Barrow***

Above: Running down over the up main from Truro into an engineering worksite at Dolcoath between Redruth and Camborne, 66546 and 66520 top-and-tail 6Y65 from Westbury past Treleigh at 10 mph on 5 December 2022. ***Craig Munday***

Above: One of only two Class 57s in Network Rail livery at the time, DRS 57305 passes Treleigh east of Redruth on 6 September 2014 with the 5E75 Penzance T&RSMD–Par empty stock, which would then form a service from Par to Exeter St Davids. This view of the line from the A3047 Redruth bypass has since been completely transformed by a new housing development. ***Keith Barrow***

Above: 9-car Class 802/1 unit 802 107 emerges from the 47 yd Redruth Tunnel and enters Redruth station with 1C80, the 12.03 Paddington–Penzance on 24 May 2023. The large building above the station is the Grade II Listed Redruth Methodist Church, which dates from 1826. *Keith Barrow*

Below: 43005 *St Michael's Mount* and 43010 *Lydford Castle* cross the 193 yd Redruth Viaduct working 2C05, the 05.40 Bristol Temple Meads–Penzance on 8 February 2023. 43005 had less than a fortnight remaining in service with GWR, working its final train on 20 February before becoming a spares donor for the Castle fleet at Plymouth Laira depot. It was moved by road from Laira to Sims Metals at Newport Docks for scrapping in July 2023. The hill on the horizon is the 630 ft St Agnes Beacon. *Finbarr O'Neill*

Above: After a day of heavy rain the clouds break over Carn Brea as 153 361 leads a Class 150/2 unit forming 2C61, the 17.55 Plymouth–Penzance through the site of Carn Brea station (closed January 1961) on 7 July 2014. A prominent local landmark, the 90 ft high Celtic cross erected as a monument to Francis Basset, 1st Baron de Dunstanville and Basset (1757–1835) is clearly visible at the summit of Carn Brea. ***Keith Barrow***

Above: Former LNER power car 43299 leads the New Measurement Train past the site of Carn Brea station working 1Q18 Reading Triangle Sidings–Paignton via Penzance on 30 July 2021. ***Keith Barrow***

Above: Royal Train loco 67006 *Royal Sovereign* passes Brea with the 1Z76 10.10 Penzance–Leeds *Cornish Riviera Statesman* on 19 April 2015. **Keith Barrow**

Above: 802 021 and 802 004 forming the late running 1C69 06.37 Paddington–Penzance meet 43194 (leading) and 43097 on 2P12 Penzance–Plymouth at Brea on 17 January 2023. Behind the trains are the remains of Cook's Kitchen Mine, which produced 40 920 tons of copper and 8859 tons of tin between the late 18th century and the 1920s. **Keith Barrow**

Above: 57603 *Tintagel Castle* crosses Brea embankment with 5Z77, the 15.20 Reading Traincare Depot–Penzance T&RSMD empty sleeper stock on 14 August 2023. ***Keith Barrow***

Above: 22 minutes into its 10h45 journey, CrossCountry *Voyager* 220 016 passes Dolcoath with 1S49, the 09.25 Penzance–Edinburgh on 16 May 2023. Immediately behind the train is the site of the former milk siding, which closed in 1983. The engine house in the background was once part of Dolcoath copper and tin mine, at its peak the largest and deepest mine in Cornwall, with the main shaft extending up to 3300 ft below ground level. ***Keith Barrow***

Above: On 5 December 2022 Freightliner 66546 arrives at Dolcoath level crossing with a train of OCA wagons carrying new sleepers, JNAs loaded with ballast, and empty JNAs for the removal of ballast from a section of the down line. 66520 was at the rear of the train, which had worked to Cornwall that morning as 6Y65 Westbury–Truro. *Keith Barrow*

Below: The immaculate interior of Roskear Junction box on 30 June 2023. *Keith Barrow*

Above: The Penzance–Paddington *Night Riviera Sleeper* pauses at Camborne with long-term DRS hire-in 57306 in charge on 28 October 2018. The car park on the left of the picture is on the site of the former goods yard. ***Nathan Stockman***

Above: Due to industrial action the only train to operate west of Truro on 3 June 2023 was an empty stock move. WCRC 47813 passes Penponds with 5Z48 Truro–Penzance *Northern Belle* ECS. Until the introduction of the Class 57/6s this loco was part of the First Great Western fleet and a regular performer on the *Night Riviera Sleeper*. ***Craig Munday***

Above: 1C83, the 13.05 Paddington–Penzance GWR service sweeps through Polmenor Downs with 43129 leading on 15 August 2017. Following the end of HST operation out of Paddington 43129 became one of 54 power cars to join the ScotRail fleet. *Keith Barrow*

Above: On 24 January 2023 43172 *Tiverton Castle* leads 2P12, the 11.15 Penzance–Plymouth through the site of Gwinear Road station, which closed on 5 October 1964. The remains of the island platform once used by branch trains to Helston are visible in the foreground. 43172 was stored on 16 August 2023 and exported to Nigeria in November 2023. *Keith Barrow*

Above: The last rays of the setting sun illuminate 57602 *Restormel Castle* as it rolls across Angarrack viaduct with 2C51, the 17.50 Exeter St Davids–Penzance on 17 June 2017. ***Keith Barrow***

Above: Fields of daffodils are a feature of the landscape in west Cornwall in early spring. The monthly visit of the Network Rail New Measurement Train to Penzance provides a suitably colour-coordinated train for this view of Angarrack Viaduct on 11 March 2016. Buffer-fitted power car 43013 is leading the train with 43062 at the rear. ***Craig Munday***

Above: 57605 *Totnes Castle* crosses Hayle Viaduct with 1C50, the 23.45 Paddington–Penzance *Night Riviera Sleeper* on 2 June 2022. In the foreground is Foundry Square, the location of Hayle's short-lived first station, which was opened by the Hayle Railway in 1844. ***Finbarr O'Neill***

Below: With only a few weeks remaining in service, celebrity power car 43185 *Great Western* leads set OC55 and 43091 forming 1A82, the 09.00 Penzance–Paddington across Hayle Viaduct on 19 April 2019. To mark the 40th anniversary of production HST operation on the Western Region 43185 was unveiled in Intercity livery in October 2016, complete with two original cast Intercity swallow logos provided by a collector. Following withdrawal from GWR service in May 2019 43185 was used as a source of spares for the ScotRail HST fleet and at the time of writing the stripped-out power car awaits its fate at Brodie Engineering in Kilmarnock. ***Keith Barrow***

Above: Just after high tide 43042 *Tregenna Castle* leads 2M77, the 19.15 Penzance–Cardiff Central across Hayle viaduct on 18 July 2023. 43042 remained active as part of the GWR fleet in January 2024. ***Keith Barrow***

Above: 153 329 crosses Hayle viaduct with an evening Plymouth–Penzance GWR service on 27 April 2017. By this time single-car Class 153 units only appeared solo on main line services in west Cornwall if the booked traction was unavailable, DMU formations usually comprising two or three vehicles. With the withdrawal of GWR's Class 153s 153 329 was transferred to the Transport for Wales fleet. ***Keith Barrow***

Above: Viewed through the signal box window, Direct Rail Services 57306 *Her Majesty's Railway Inspectorate 175* arrives at St Erth with 1C99, the 23.50 Paddington–Penzance *Night Riviera Sleeper* on 17 August 2019. ***Craig Munday***

Above: 43029 *Caldicot Castle* leads 2C77, the 13.14 Newport–Penzance into St Erth on 16 May 2023. The track layout at this end of the station was rationalised in November 2014 with the removal of two sidings opposite the signal box behind the train. The signal on the far left guards the St Ives branch. The operation of HSTs on GWR services from South Wales to Cornwall ended in December 2023 and these duties are now in the hands of IETs. ***Joshua Barrow***

Above: Colas Rail 43274, the sole HST power car to receive East Midlands Railway livery, leads the New Measurement Train through St Erth working 1Q18 05.53 Reading Triangle Sidings–Paignton via Penzance on 2 June 2023. 43272 is at the rear of the train. The station is deserted due to a strike.

In early 2024 work was underway on a new footbridge just to to west of the current structure, which will be equipped with lifts to provide step-free access to all platforms. The current bridge will be removed and rebuilt at Cranmore station on the East Somerset Railway. ***Keith Barrow***

Above: 221 131 passes the recently cleared embankments at Rospeath on the climb from Penzance towards St Erth with 1S47, the 08.37 Penzance–Edinburgh on 25 May 2023. The distant signal for the single-track section between Marazion and Long Rock is visible on the down line.

This was the first week of the 2023 summer timetable, which saw two CrossCountry departures from Penzance, at 06.28 and 08.37, both for Edinburgh. ***Nathan Stockman***

Above: On 31 May 2014 43025 leading 1C72, the 06.44 Bristol Temple Meads–Penzance came to a stand while pulling away from Truro station. The train set back into the station and was eventually dumped in the yard to await rescue. 57602 *Restormel Castle* wastherefore taken off 2E75, the 11.25 Par–Exeter St Davids at Plymouth and ran light engine to Truro to collect the errant HST and haul it to Long Rock. The formation is pictured at Rosevidney running as 5Z72 15.50 Truro–Penzance T&RSMD. That evening the Class 57 dragged the HST from Penzance to Plymouth Laira depot for attention, returning to Penzance the following day with the stock from 2E75. However, this was not achieved without more drama as difficulty getting 57602 started at Plymouth station resulted in that evening's sleeper to Paddington departing Penzance 57 minutes late! *Craig Munday*

Below: On 31 March 2017 a heavy shower in the Penzance area provides a dramatic backdrop for 43037 *Penydarren* as it leads 1A83 to Paddington away from the terminus. The train is passing the site of Marazion station, which closed on 5 October 1964, although the building on the former down platform survives. Following withdrawal by GWR 43037 joined the ScotRail fleet. *Craig Munday*

Above: 70817 stands outside the new depot building at Long Rock on 20 March 2018 with an engineering train, which was on site in connection with the relaying of the single-track main line adjacent to the depot. *Nathan Stockman*

Above: Four Castle HST sets and 57603 *Tintagel Castle* on a train of sleeper stock line up in the sidings at Long Rock depot beneath a full moon on 8 April 2020. By this time, it was unusual not to find at least one IET stabled overnight in the yard. *Craig Munday*

Above: Late morning at Long Rock on 22 May 2023 and 57605 *Totnes Castle* ticks over inside the shed as depot pilot 08645 rests in the yard. The Class 08 is named *St Piran* after the patron saint of tin miners and carries a unique livery based on the Cornish flag, which was unveiled at the Long Rock open day on 13 April 2019. *Keith Barrow*

Above: 57602 *Restormel Castle* on the jacks inside Long Rock depot on 13 April 2019. *Keith Barrow*

Above: Network Rail's New Measurement Train passes Ponsandane on the final approach to Penzance forming 1Q18, the 05.25 Old Oak Common–Paignton via Penzance on 21 October 2016. 43062 was leading with 43014 (nearest the camera) at the rear. *Keith Barrow*

Above: During the upgrading of Long Rock depot the spare *Night Riviera Sleeper* coaches could often be found stabled in Slopers Siding at Ponsandane between the depot and Penzance station, where 08410 is pictured on 11 December 2016. Behind the loco is Mark 1 barrier coach 6348. 08410 is now owned by AV Dawson and is used for shunting at the Ayrton Rail Terminal in Middlesborough, but retains its GWR green livery. *Nathan Stockman*

Above: 43041 *St Catherine's Castle* leads 2C31, the 15.55 from Plymouth into Penzance station on 18 June 2021. 43004 is at the rear of the train. The following summer 43041 had the unfortunate distinction of being the first Castle HST power car to be withdrawn. Stored on 14 August 2022 as it was due both an F exam and an engine overhaul, 43041 was used as a source of spares for the Castle fleet at Plymouth Laira depot before being moved by road to the Sims scrapyard at Newport Docks in July 2023. *Mark Lynam*

Below: A June 2022 aerial view of the station showing most of the main passenger train types used in Cornwall in the early 2020s, with a Class 150 DMU in the sidings on the left, A CrossCountry Class 220 *Voyager* in Platform 4, a GWR Castle HST in Platform 3, a Hitachi-built IET bi-mode unit in Platform 2 and the *Night Riviera Sleeper* Mark 3 stock in Platform 1. *Finbarr O'Neill*

Above: Long Rock depot pilot 08645 *St Piran* powers away from Platform 1 at Penzance with the empty stock of the *Night Riviera Sleeper* from Paddington on 4 May 2023. Usually, the Class 57 that has hauled the train from Paddington propels the empty stock back towards Ponsandane, where the loco runs round before proceeding to the depot at Long Rock. **Craig Munday**

Above: Our journey along the Cornish Main Line ends with the classic view of Penzance station from Chyandour Cliff. On 9 May 2023 CrossCountry 43289 and InterCity "Executive" liveried 43184 have arrived with 1Z58, the 16.45 Bristol Temple Meads–Penzance, which ran in place of the usual *Voyager* due to flooding in the Bristol area, and are awaiting departure with 2C80, the 22.08 Penzance–Plymouth. This would be the final CrossCountry HST working in Cornwall before the withdrawal of the fleet in September 2023. On the right 57603 *Tintagel Castle* heads 1A40, the *Night Riviera Sleeper* to Paddington. **Mark Lynam**

INDEX

Above: To highlight the requirement for passengers to wear facemasks during the Covid-19 pandemic, IET set 800 321 was adorned with "facemask" vinyls on both driving cars. These were retained for some time after the restrictions were lifted. On 28 May 2022 the bi-mode unit passes Bethany with 1C79, the 11:38 Paddington–Newquay. *Nathan Stockman*